Cooking with Herbs

100 SEASONAL RECIPES AND HERBAL MIXTURES TO SPICE UP ANY MEAL

Tina James

RODALE

With blessings to the many adventurous
eaters who have cheered me on,
and a big squeeze to George, my husband
and faithful sous-chef

**WE INSPIRE AND ENABLE PEOPLE TO IMPROVE
THEIR LIVES AND THE WORLD AROUND THEM**

Storey Books:
Editor: Gwen W. Steege
Text Designer: Eugenie Seidenberg Delaney
Cover Designer: Meredith Maker
Text Illustrators: All illustrations by Beverly K. Duncan with the exception of those by Brigita Fuhrmann, pages 27, 36, 54, 74, 128 (bottom), 129, 131 (bottom), 132, 137, and 142 (top); Sarah Brill, pages 30, 67, 72, 124, 125 (top), 134, 138, and 146; Charles Joslin, pages 47, 57, 63, 77, 87, 89, 125 (top), 130, 131 (top), 133, 136, 142 (bottom), 143–45; Regina Hughes, page 48; and Mallory Lake, pages 128 (top) and 139.
Production Assistant: Susan Bernier
Indexer: Susan Olason, Indexes and Knowledge Maps

Rodale Organic Gardening Books:
Executive Editor: Ellen Phillips
Editor: Karen Costello Soltys
Executive Creative Director: Christin Gangi
Art Director and Cover Designer: Patricia Field
Cover Illustrator: Mia Bosna
Studio Manager: Leslie Keefe
Manufacturing Manager: Mark Krahforst

For questions or comments concerning the editorial content of this book, please write to:
Rodale
Book Readers' Service
33 East Minor Street
Emmaus, PA 18098
For more information about Rodale and the books and magazines we publish, visit our World Wide Web site at:
http://www.rodale.com

Library of Congress Cataloging-in-Publication Data
James, Tina, date
    Cooking with herbs : 100 seasonal recipes and herbal mixtures to spice up any meal / Tina James.
        p.   cm. — (Rodale's essential herbal handbooks)
    Includes index.
    ISBN 0–87596–811–2 (hardcover)   ISBN 0–87596–829–5 (pbk.)
    1. Cookery (Herbs) 2. Herbs. 3. Herb gardening. I. Title. II. Series.
    TX819.H4 J25 1999
    641.6'57—dc21

Distributed in the book trade by St. Martin's Press
Printed in the United States
2 4 6 8 10 9 7 5 3 1 hardcover
2 4 6 8 10 9 7 5 3 1 paperback

Contents

CHAPTER 6 (CONTINUED)

CHAPTER 7: COOKING HERBS A TO Z 123

HERBAL RESOURCES 147

INDEX 150

CHAPTER 1

YOUR ESSENTIAL
Herbal Pantry

Chocolate pudding was my first signature dish and my dear daddy was kind enough to savor it. Buoyed by early acclaim, I've licked many pots and now stir without standing on a stool. My rules for cooking have been distilled over the years to a simple maxim that translates to living as well. I want the food I serve to be beautiful and nourishing: that is, to delight the eye, smell divine, taste scrumptious, and satisfy completely. Using herbs artfully with garden-fresh ingredients is the best way I know to prepare delightful food. Just breathing in the fragrance of basil and rosemary inspires homage to the simple pleasures that bring joy to each day. And, as a little girl discovered long ago, something good to eat and a few kind words carry us a long way down the road.

1

EXPLORING THE POSSIBILITIES OF HERBAL COOKING

Nothing compares to the aroma of chopping spicy-fresh marjoram or mincing a bunch of pungent dill. Think about zesting a lemon and the burst of essential oil that you can taste without its entering your mouth. Fresh herbs give food that same lively zip without overpowering the taste buds. In addition to fresh herb leaves and blossoms, some recipes in this book call for herb seeds like cumin, and spices like cinnamon and cloves. In this introductory chapter, you'll find many suggestions for incorporating herbs into your daily cooking, as well as some basic recipes for herb blends, butters, teas, honeys, and jellies.

MATCHING HERBS TO FOODS

Certain herbs seem to have a love affair with particular foods. Who can argue that tomatoes and basil are a perfect match? If you're new to cooking with herbs, take time to identify the flavor of individual herbs. Crush a leaf of savory between your fingers and enjoy the scent. What comes to mind? If your background is German, where savory and green beans go hand in hand, your immediate association may very well be green beans! Nibble on a cinnamon basil leaf. What does it taste like? Close your eyes and try to imagine what foods each of these herb flavors will enhance. Now begin to experiment in the kitchen. Mince a few leaves and use them in dishes where their flavor will stand out, such as a simple salad or an omelet, a cup of tea, or buttered toast. You'll soon be able to create from a whole repertoire of fresh flavor combinations.

The Herb-Food Partnerships chart on page 4 suggests some herb-food marriages made in heaven. After experimenting with these combinations and finding some favorites, take a creative leap and explore inspirations that come to you.

The tomato-basil flavor "marriage" seems to have been made in heaven.

THE ALLURE OF FRESH HERBS

Fresh herbs, such as parsley, chives, cilantro, basil, and dill, are much preferred over dried herbs for garnishing dishes like salads, omelets, salsas, and vegetables. I'm able to grow most of my own culinary herbs and can harvest something fresh in all but the coldest months in my Zone 6b growing area. To prolong the supply, I bring the rosemary and bay indoors. I also mulch the thyme, chives, Italian parsley, and mint with shredded oak leaves. With a little luck, I can usually find fresh pickings until Christmas.

> ### Lively Spices
>
> For freshest flavor, buy whole seeds and spices and grind them in a coffee grinder before adding them to a recipe.

If you're making pesto, fresh herbs are essential. Fortunately, these herbs are easy to grow, and if you don't garden, many markets now stock fresh basil, as well as Italian parsley, cilantro, dill, and watercress. All of these make excellent — and super nutritious — pesto.

But even if you love to garden, you probably can't grow all of the herbs and spices you'll need for cooking throughout the year. Some herbs need a long, warm growing season (cumin and sesame seed, for example) and are difficult to grow in most parts of North America. If garden space is limited, grow the herbs you enjoy using fresh, especially those that you need in such large quantity that they would be expensive to buy. Organically grown Italian parsley, dill, and cilantro are now available at many groceries for a modest price. Purchase those herbs, and use the saved garden space for basil or marjoram, which may be more costly or harder to find fresh. Or, devote extra space to mint or tarragon, which are needed in abundance for vinegar making.

Large quantities of herbs like fresh basil and parsley are essential for pesto making.

Herb-Food Partnerships

HERB	CHARACTERISTICS	COMPLEMENTARY FOODS
Basil	Clovelike flavor with a hint of mint	Tomatoes, corn, zucchini, green salads, cheese and other dairy dishes, chicken, fish
Bay	Spicy evergreen flavor	Soups and stews, poached fish, pasta sauce; add a bay leaf to the water when cooking noodles or other pasta
Chervil	Delicate parsley flavor with a hint of anise	Eggs, fish, shellfish, asparagus, peas, potatoes, beets
Chives	Mild onion flavor	Cold soups; dairy-based dips, spreads, and dressings; vegetables; eggs
Garlic chives	Mild garlic flavor	Garlic substitute, stir-fries, salads
Cilantro	Earthy, sagey, citrusy (detractors claim it tastes "soapy")	Spicy (Indian, Mexican, and Thai) cuisines, in dishes such as salsa, curry, chili; counters highly seasoned foods
Dill	Sweet and tangy	Hot and cold fish, yogurts, soups, dips, beans, cabbage, pickles, and cold salads like shrimp, potato, and cucumber
Marjoram	Sweet oregano-like flavor	Chicken, most summer vegetables (peas, summer squash, beans, corn, and tomatoes)
Mint	Sweet and pungent	Yogurt dishes, peas, carrots, fruit salads; traditionally associated with lamb
Oregano	Assertive peppery flavor	Highly seasoned dishes, tomato-based preparations; associated with Greek and Italian cuisines
Parsley	Fresh flavor	Almost any dish that isn't sweet; very nutritious; Italian flat-leaved parsley more flavorful; curly parsley for garnishing
Sage	Smoky flavor, somewhat bitter	Poultry stuffing, succotash; associated with wild game
Savory	Peppery	Beans, summer squash, vegetable soups
Tarragon	Distinctive anise flavor	French cuisine (vinaigrette dressing and béarnaise sauce), chicken, fish, meats, potatoes, asparagus, beets, spinach
Thyme	Fresh lemony flavor with a spicy aftertaste	French cuisine, eggs, cheese, poultry, fish, meats, soups, cream sauces, onions, peas, mushrooms

WHEN YOU DON'T HAVE FRESH HERBS

Although nothing compares to the aroma of chopping fresh basil, dried or frozen herbs stand in nicely for fresh herbs during the winter months. Preserving your own herbs is easy (see page 111) and gives one the primal satisfaction of stocking up for the cold months ahead. You can also buy good quality dried herbs. I've found the highest quality herbs from health-food stores, gourmet produce shops, and mail-order suppliers. (See page 147.)

The cost is very reasonable if you buy in bulk rather than pay for fancy packaging. The criteria for selection is simple: The herbs should smell fresh and, if they're from green plants, they should be bright green in color.

KNOWING AN HERB FROM A SPICE

What's the difference between an herb and a spice? Herbs and spices are both derived from plants and are valued for their use and delight. All or one part of the plant may be used — the root, stem, leaf, flower, fruits (seeds or seedpods) — and with spices, the bark as well. In general, herbs are herbaceous or green plants, plants whose stems are soft rather than woody. Herbaceous plants typically die down to the ground or even to the roots at the end of the growing season. In the United States, we think of herbs as growing in temperate zones; we think of spices as coming from tropical climes.

Spices are often good complements for cooking with herbs, and many of the recipes in this book include spices or spice mixtures, such as curry powder. Stocking Up on Herbs and Spices on page 6 lists some of the spices, as well as herb seeds, that you may want to stock up on.

Store seeds and spices in airtight containers in a cool, dark place, not over the stove! Store fresh gingerroot in the refrigerator for one or two weeks. For long-term storage, cut the root into thick slices and place them in a glass jar. Cover with apple cider vinegar or white wine vinegar — no need to refrigerate. When you're ready to use them, pat them dry and proceed with your recipe.

Herb seeds, like cumin, sesame, poppy, and coriander, need a little coaxing to bring out their best flavor. Toast seeds in a small heavy skillet for several minutes on low heat. Shake the pan once or twice to warm the seeds evenly. When you can smell the fragrance of the seeds, toss them once more and they're done. (They don't need to brown.) Remove seeds from heat and allow them to cool. Grind seeds with a mortar and pestle, or a coffee grinder for larger amounts. Grinding seeds immediately before use results in much fresher flavor.

USING HERBS IN YOUR COOKING

Ready to make a green salad with fresh herbs? Let's use garlic chives, marjoram, and parsley. Shake the herbs into the sink. If you see any dirt, rinse the herbs quickly under cool water and shake. Spin the herbs in a salad spinner to dry — or wrap them loosely in a towel or pillowcase and go outside and shake them hard.

MINCING METHODS

Scissors work well for mincing in most instances. To mince the blades of herbs like garlic chives, hold a small bunch of them over the salad or a bowl and snip into tiny pieces using sharp kitchen scissors. For soft-stalked herbs like parsley, dill, and cilantro, you needn't strip

Stocking Up on Herbs and Spices

In addition to fresh and dried herbs, you may want to stock up on these herb seeds and spices:

- Ground cinnamon
- Cinnamon sticks
- Cumin seed
- Curry powder
- Ground ginger
- Fresh gingerroot

- Whole nutmeg
- Hungarian paprika
- Ground cayenne pepper
- Black or mixed peppercorns
- Whole or ground white pepper
- Sesame seed

the leaves; simply trim away tough stems, roll the leaves into a small ball, and then take tiny snips, cutting right through the ball.

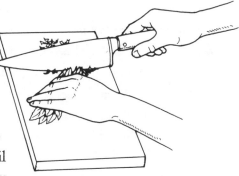

Roll several leaves into a small ball, then snip with scissors or a knife.

For woody-stemmed herbs like marjoram, thyme, sage, and rosemary, strip the leaves from the stems (unless the stems are very tender, in which case you can treat them as you do parsley), cut the herbs coarsely with scissors into a teacup, then cut them against the sides of the cup until the greens are finely minced. I like to sprinkle minced herbs directly on the salad, but you can also add them to a salad dressing.

Use scissors to mince herb leaves in a teacup.

For a large quantity of herbs, it may be easier and faster to use a sharp chef's knife and cutting board than scissors. Remove the stems or strip the leaves as described above, and lay the leaves flat on the board. Use one hand to position the leaves and the other to chop. In most cases, it's best to "mince fine," that is, chop until the herbs are cut into tiny bits. Coarse chopping will do if the herbs are to be pureed, as in pesto.

Mince large bundles of herbs on a cutting board.

Some people use a food processor to mince fresh herbs. Unless you're very careful, however, machines can turn tender herbs into mush. And then you have to clean the machine! It's just not worth it for small amounts. I do use a standard-size food processor for pesto, however, and a coffee grinder to grind dry herbs.

How to Measure Herbs

- Mound dried herbs on the measuring spoon. Then use your fingers to crumble them into foods.
- Measure ground herbs by the level spoonful.
- Pack minced fresh herbs to measure.
- Use two to three times more fresh herbs when substituting them for dried herbs in a recipe. Use the lower end of the range for strongly flavored herbs like rosemary and sage.
- To substitute dried herbs for fresh, crush a few leaves in your hands. If they smell very fresh, use one-third as much. If the aroma is faint, use half as much. Fresh herbs are unlikely to overpower a dish, but it's better to err on the side of caution with dried herbs.

WHEN TO ADD FRESH HERBS

Mix fresh herbs into salad dressings and sauces and use them to garnish the final presentation as well. In cooked dishes, add the woodier fresh herbs (sage, thyme, rosemary, tarragon) during the last half hour of cooking. If you're using delicate herbs like cilantro, basil, dill, chives, marjoram, or parsley, stir them into the dish a minute or two before serving. When I make soups, I often put freshly minced herbs in the bottom of each soup bowl and then ladle the soup over the herbs. The hot liquid infuses the herb and captures its fresh flavor.

WHEN TO ADD DRIED HERBS

Ground herbs have a more intense flavor and dissolve into the food, so diners won't notice the texture of the dried leaves. If you have whole or crumbled dried herbs, rub them between your fingers or zip them (singly or in a blend; see page 9) in a coffee grinder until they are finely ground. Once ground, the flavorful essential oils dissipate rapidly, so prepare ground herbs in small batches and use them within a month.

For salad dressings and sauces, add the dried herbs and let stand at least 10 minutes in order to rehydrate the herb and to allow flavors to mingle. For cooked dishes like soups and stews, add woody herbs when assembling the ingredients. Crumble the herbs with your fingers. If you're using more delicate herbs, add them 10 to 15 minutes before serving, again crumbling the leaves with your fingers.

EQUIPPING YOUR KITCHEN FOR HERB COOKERY

The bare-bones list of supplies includes a pair of sharp scissors that feel comfortable in your hand for mincing herbs, a chef's knife for chopping herbs and garlic, and a mortar and pestle for grinding seeds and herb blends. Although for centuries cooks made pesto using only a mortar and pestle, a food processor is much faster. Faster isn't always better, though — the noise certainly isn't soothing — but I confess to using the modern method here. I also rely on a coffee grinder to grind large amounts of seeds and dried herbs. By the way, don't try to use the same gadget for grinding coffee and herbs. Both leave indelible flavors that resist even the most ardent attempts at cleaning. To clean, wipe the reservoir with a paper towel after each use. A small food processor is another option, but it doesn't grind as uniformly as a coffee grinder.

Culinary scissors and a chef's knife are indispensable tools.

COMBINING HERBAL FLAVORS

Although any herb can stand alone, blended herbs develop more complex flavors. Begin your experimenting by composing a tried-and-true herb blend as a springboard. The classic French mixture called *fines herbes* consists of chives (onion family), chervil (carrot family), thyme (mint family), and often tarragon. Each "family" of herbs shares similar flavor characteristics. (See Flavor Families on page 10.) You can play with the basic fines herbes formula, combining one or more herbs from each family to produce dozens of variations.

Flavor Families

Onion family. Chives, garlic chives, garlic, leek, bulb onions, scallions (or green onions), shallots
Carrot family. Anise, caraway, celery, chervil, cilantro/coriander, cumin, dill, fennel, lovage, parsley. Use seeds or leaves for different flavors.
Mint family. Basil, lemon balm, marjoram, mints, oregano, rosemary, sage, savory, thyme

A few oddballs seem to refuse to fit neatly in any category. Although anise-flavored tarragon, in the composite family, combines with the onion family and neutral herbs like parsley and thyme, it's best on its own. Bay leaves, in the laurel family, have a mildly spicy evergreen flavor, good in soups and stews; bay blends with many herbs.

BOUQUET GARNI

A *bouquet garni* is a small bunch of fresh herbs gathered together with string (or tied up in a piece of muslin or an unbleached

Tuck a bunch of fresh herbs into a napkin ring.

coffee filter) and dropped into soups and stews during the last half hour of cooking. A *bouquet garni* needs no chopping and is easy to fish out of the pot after cooking. Although a bouquet garni is usually used for cooking, a fresh one is also pretty inserted into napkin rings!

A standard bouquet consists of a bay leaf, a few sprigs of thyme, two or three parsley stalks, and often a sprig of tarragon. Vary the combination of herbs in your bouquet according to the foods in the dish. Here are some suggestions to start with:

With vegetables: parsley, savory, thyme, and bay
With chicken: marjoram, rosemary, and savory; fennel, rosemary, and bay; parsley, bay, and lemongrass
With turkey: sage, bay, and parsley
With fish: tarragon and parsley; fennel, bay, and lemon thyme; dill, parsley, and mint

A FEW ALL-PURPOSE HERB BLENDS

I don't make many dried herb blends because I prefer to smell and taste while adding each ingredient. The following combinations are so versatile, however, that it's worth preparing a month's supply. They're also handy for doctoring prepared foods.

The instructions for each mix are the same: Simply combine all ingredients and then store in airtight containers. Crumble or grind the herbs when adding them to foods. Mixes are best used within three to six months.

Poultry Seasoning

The herbs in this traditional mixture are tried-and-true seasonings for roasting chicken and livening up stuffing. I use them in Uncle Bicky's Not-Red Barbecue Chicken (page 37). Poultry Seasoning also enlivens steamed vegetables, rice, and stir-fries. Makes ½ cup.

> 3 tablespoons lemon thyme
>
> 2 tablespoons marjoram
>
> 1 tablespoon sage
>
> 1 tablespoon rosemary
>
> 2 teaspoons freshly ground black pepper
>
> ½ teaspoon nutmeg

Italian Seasoning

Mediterranean herbs are a great way to entice "just meat-and-potato eaters" down the herbal path. Use this savory blend to perk up tomato sauce, pizza sauce, roasted vegetables, and salad dressing. Makes about ½ cup.

> 3 tablespoons basil
>
> 2 tablespoons oregano or marjoram
>
> 1 tablespoon thyme
>
> 2 teaspoons rosemary

Sesame Salt

This simple seasoning is excellent on steamed vegetables and grains like rice and quinoa. Shake the pan occasionally while toasting the seeds to avoid burning them.

> 8 parts sesame seeds
> 1 part sea salt or kosher salt

1. Dry-toast the sesame seeds over medium-low heat in a heavy skillet until fragrant.
2. Grind the sesame seeds with the salt with a mortar and pestle or coffee grinder.
3. Store in an airtight container in the refrigerator. Use within three months.

No-Salt Sesame Herb Blend

This full-flavored salt blend is made with calcium-rich sesame and mineral-rich herbs and kelp, a type of seaweed. Kelp powder is available in health-food stores. Many health-food stores also carry dried wild herbs like dandelion and nettles. (See also Mail-Order Resources, page 147.) Makes about 1½ cups.

> 1 cup sesame seeds
> 2 tablespoons garlic powder
> 1 tablespoon dried rosemary
> 1 tablespoon dried marjoram
> 1 tablespoon dried lemon thyme
> 1 tablespoon dried dandelion leaf
> 1 tablespoon dried nettle leaf
> 2 teaspoons savory
> 2 teaspoons kelp powder

1. Dry-toast the sesame seeds over medium-low heat in a heavy skillet until fragrant. Cool slightly.
2. Grind the seeds with the herbs.
3. Store in an airtight container in the refrigerator. Use within three months.

Sweet Potato Unfries

Here's a tasty and nutritious snack with very little fat. Preheat the oven to 425°F. Spray a baking sheet with nonstick cooking spray. Scrub some sweet potatoes but do not peel them. Cut the potatoes into ⅛-inch slices. Place them in a single layer on the baking sheet, and brush them lightly with olive oil. Sprinkle generously with Cajun Blend (recipe below). Bake for 15 minutes. Turn the slices and bake 5 minutes more. Enjoy this spicy treat hot.

Cajun Blend

The sweet and spicy zest of this Cajun mixture is ideal for seasoning fish and chicken before grilling. It's also good on popcorn. Makes about 1¼ cups.

> 5 tablespoons paprika
> 5 tablespoons thyme
> 2 tablespoons oregano or marjoram
> 2 tablespoons freshly ground black pepper
> 2 tablespoons garlic powder
> 1 tablespoon kosher salt (optional)
> 1 tablespoon cayenne pepper
> 1 teaspoon cumin seed
> 1 teaspoon ground ginger
> ½ teaspoon ground cloves

HERB BUTTERS

Combining fresh herbs and unsalted butter creates a versatile seasoning for cooked vegetables, hot breads, soups and chowders, and baked fish. Plus, it really perk up canned soups and frozen vegetables. Herb butters also freeze well, so this is an excellent way to preserve garden-fresh flavors — particularly chervil and dill, which don't dry well.

As a general rule, use 5 tablespoons of minced fresh herbs to 1 stick of softened unsalted (sweet) butter. Blend well and refrigerate in an airtight container for up to ten days, or freeze for longer storage. Use your favorite individual herbs or combine flavors. See Herb-Butter Partnerships, below, for some favorite combinations to get you started.

If you're trying to lower cholesterol, make Better Butter. Combine ½ cup cold-pressed vegetable oil with ½ cup softened, unsalted butter. Then use the Herb-Butter combinations below. Better Butter freezes well, too. (Cold-pressed vegetable oil is extracted by methods that don't involve heat, thereby preserving important nutrients like vitamin E. Use this oil in recipes that you don't cook, such as herb butters or salad dressings. It's available in health-food stores and gourmet shops.)

Herb-Butter Partnerships

HERBS	USES
Equal parts parsley, chervil, and chives	All-purpose
Equal parts dill, chervil, and chives	All-purpose
Equal parts burnet or borage, chervil, and chives	All-purpose
Equal parts lemon balm, chives, and parsley	Fish, vegetables
Equal parts chervil, chives, and mint	Fish, carrots, peas
Equal parts marjoram and basil	Chicken, peas, carrots, corn, squash
Equal parts calendula petals, chives, and parsley	Pretty on vegetables and rice
2 parts nasturtium flowers, to 1 part nasturtium leaves, to ½ teaspoon of lemon juice	Hot breads; great cucumber sandwich spread!
Scented geranium flowers, rose petals, or dianthus blossoms	Scones, waffles, muffins
Calamint (Calamintha nepeta) blossoms with a squeeze of lemon juice (calamint blossoms have a delightful peppery-mint flavor)	Delicious on peas, mushrooms, carrots, biscuits
Mixed herb and flower blossoms (such as thyme, chicory, borage, calendula, 'Lemon Gem' marigold, opal basil, lavender, carnation, clove pinks)	Beautiful for biscuits, scones

Herb Mustard

YIELD: 2¼ CUPS

My friend Nancy Taylor Robson, author of *Oldfield Lamb Cookbook*, introduced me to homemade mustard. You can vary by using different herbs and vinegars. Nancy uses curry plant *(Helichrysum angustifolium)* or curry powder and part sherry. I opt for tarragon. Thyme is good with red-wine-based herb vinegars. The sharp mustard flavor mellows after a week or two.

> 1 cup ground mustard
> 2 teaspoons salt
> ¾ cup tarragon vinegar (made with rice or white wine vinegar)
> ½ cup water
> ¾ cup honey
> 1 teaspoon dried tarragon
> 2 beaten eggs

1. Mix all ingredients except the eggs in the top of a double boiler. Let stand for several hours before heating.
2. Bring the water in the double boiler to a boil. Whisk the mustard ingredients until the mixture begins to thicken. Gradually add the eggs, whisking continuously. Cook over boiling water for 10 minutes. The mustard will be fairly thickened by then, and it will thicken more as it sets.
3. Pour into sterilized jars and refrigerate.

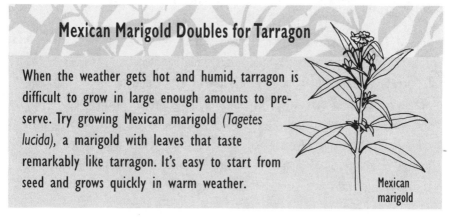

Mexican Marigold Doubles for Tarragon

When the weather gets hot and humid, tarragon is difficult to grow in large enough amounts to preserve. Try growing Mexican marigold *(Tagetes lucida)*, a marigold with leaves that taste remarkably like tarragon. It's easy to start from seed and grows quickly in warm weather.

Mexican marigold

HERB TEAS

Herb teas are a pleasant "decaf" beverage and offer endless variety. The eleven all-purpose blends below work well for both fresh and dried herbs. Feel free to add herbs to black or decaf tea. Then be sure to see A Perfect Pot of Herb Tea (at right) for brewing directions.

- 4 parts rosemary and 1 part lavender (good hot or iced with Earl Grey tea!)
- 2 parts lemon balm and 1 part sage
- 2 parts peppermint and 1 part yarrow
- 1 part lemon verbena and 1 part bergamot flowers
- 1 part mint and 1 part alfalfa
- 4 parts spearmint, 2 parts chamomile, and 1 part rosemary
- 1 part thyme, 1 part bergamot flowers, and a pinch of ground ginger
- 2 parts linden flowers, 1 part rosemary, and 1 part gingerroot
- 1 part peppermint, 1 part basil, and 1 part thyme
- 2 parts marjoram, 1 part mint, and a little orange peel
- 8 parts spearmint, 4 parts peppermint, 4 parts anise hyssop, 1 part sage, and 1 part rosemary

Super Sweet Stevia

Stevia (*Stevia rebaudiana*) is the sweetest natural product yet discovered, 10 to 15 times sweeter by volume than sugar. Two or three leaves will sweeten 4 to 6 cups of tea, and has little effect on other herb flavors. This Zone 9 herb is easy to grow in a pot and to propagate by seed or cuttings. It can also be grown as an annual; the leaves are easy to dry. The best news is that stevia contains virtually no calories, does not adversely affect blood sugar levels, and causes no known ill effects. South American cultures have used the herb for centuries. (For plant and seed sources, see page 147.)

Stevia

A Perfect Pot of Herb Tea

Here's how to make a perfect pot of tea. It takes only a few extra minutes to enjoy much more flavor, and the whole process, like the tea itself, is satisfying and relaxing. You'll need two china or glass teapots, one for brewing, the other for serving, and a bamboo or wire-mesh strainer.

> Freshly boiled water (spring or distilled water is best)
> 1 heaping tablespoon fresh herbs *or* 1 mounded teaspoon dried
>   herbs per cup of boiling water
> Lemon and honey (optional)

1. Heat the water and pour a little into both teapots to warm them.
2. Empty the water from the brewing pot, measure the herbs into it, and then pour boiling water over them. Cover the pot and let tea steep for 5 minutes.
3. Empty the hot water out of the serving pot. Pour the tea through a strainer into the serving pot or directly into warmed teacups. Serve with the optional lemon and honey.

Easy Homemade Tea Filter

Crumbling herbs into tea bags dissipates essential oils and greatly shortens storage life. Brewing tea with "loose" dried herbs doesn't have to be complicated, however, when you use this easy-to-make tea "filter" fashioned from an unbleached round coffee filter. To make, fold the filter in half. Then fold it in thirds toward the middle to form a cone. When you open the cone, you have a leakproof filter. Pierce two holes in the edge of the cone as shown, and insert a dried herb stalk or skewer through the holes to support the filter in the cup. Voilà! Tea filters can be reused several times before composting.

Tonic Teas

Herb teas can be more than a refreshing beverage. Some varieties can help you treat specific health problems. Consult a book on herbal remedies (see page 149) for advice on which herbs are most effective for which conditions. In addition, you can brew tonic teas, which are simply strong infusions of food-quality herbs brewed for a longer period than regular tea so as to extract all the nutrients. They are designed to be an integral part of a health maintenance program. To keep you feeling healthy, try this tonic tea recipe. Prepare a large jarful of this mixture and use it immediately, or store it, covered tightly, in a cool, dark place for up to six months. Or, make the blend with fresh herbs for immediate use.

2 parts dried peppermint — rich in calcium
1 part dried oatstraw (Avena sativa) — nerve strengthener
1 part dried nettle (Urtica dioica) — rich in iron, chlorophyll, and amino acids
1 part dried chickweed (Stellaria media) — rich in minerals, especially silica
1 part dried red clover heads (Trifolium pratense) — good blood cleanser
1 part dried alfalfa leaf — rich in iron, vitamins, and minerals
½ part dried lemon balm — calming and calcium-rich
¼ part dried chamomile — good digestive

1. Place 2 heaping tablespoons of the dried herb mixture (6 to 8 tablespoons of fresh herbs) in a 2-quart, heatproof container. Fill with boiling water.
2. Cover the container with a folded tea towel. To gather all the goodness, let sit at least 2 hours before drinking. (I let mine sit overnight.) Refrigerate if not consumed within 8 hours. You can flavor the tea with lemon, honey, or both if you wish.

Herb Jellies

Herb jelly is a delicate delight to spread on any hot bread. You can also use it in glazes or marinades. Because the basic recipe calls for infusing the jelly with fresh herbs twice, the result is extra flavorful. See page 20 for suggestions for herb and liquid combinations. The basic recipe makes 6 cups.

BASIC METHOD FOR MAKING HERB JELLY

2 cups boiling water

2 cups packed fresh herb leaves

2½ cups (approximately) unsweetened apple juice

3½ cups granulated sugar

1 package Sure-Gel or other low-sugar pectin

2 cups fresh herb sprigs

4 tablespoons cider vinegar

1 herb sprig for each jar, for garnish

1. Wash six half-pint or three one-pint canning jars and jar rings in the dishwasher or in hot soapy water. Rinse well. Place jars, rings, and new vacuum lids in gently boiling water until you are ready for them.
2. Pour the boiling water over the fresh herb leaves; infuse for 1 hour. Strain. Measure the infusion into a large saucepan. Add enough apple juice to make 4½ cups total liquid.
3. In a small bowl, mix ¼ cup of the sugar with the pectin. Whisk into herb infusion, and bring to a rolling boil. Stir in remaining sugar; return to a boil. Boil hard for 1 full minute. Remove from the heat. Stir in 2 cups fresh herb sprigs. Cover; let steep for 5 minutes.
4. With tongs, pull out the herbs. Skim off the foam. Stir in the vinegar.
5. Place a small fresh herb sprig in each jar. Fill with jelly to within ¼ inch of rim. Wipe rims with a clean cloth, cover with vacuum lid, and secure with metal ring. Load jars into canning kettle half filled with hot water. Add water to reach at least 2 inches above jar tops. Bring water to a boil and boil gently for 10 minutes. Remove jars; cool completely. Store up to one year in a cool, dark place.

Herb Jelly Variations

You can customize your herb jelly in a variety of ways. Use the basic jelly recipe on page 19 as your starting point and try one of the following variations. As you gain confidence, you'll come up with any number of creative new recipes.

- Use fruit juice for the herb infusion (step 2), instead of the 2 cups of water.
- Replace the 2½ cups apple juice with other unsweetened liquids like apple cider, white grape juice, grapefruit juice, or cranberry juice.
- Use lemon juice in place of the cider vinegar, depending on the flavor of the herb.

Here are some suggestions for combinations of herbs and juices to get you started. (Use the same amounts of sugar and Sure-Gel or other low-sugar pectin as specified by the basic recipe.)

HERB	LIQUID (WATER/JUICE)	VINEGAR/LEMON JUICE
2 cups mint leaves	2 cups boiling water and 2½ cups apple juice	4 tablespoons cider vinegar
2 cups basil leaves (cinnamon and holy basil, for instance)	2 cups boiling water and 2½ cups apple juice	4 tablespoons vinegar
1 cup sage leaves	2 cups boiling water and 2½ cups apple cider	4 tablespoons vinegar
1 cup savory leaves	4½ cups grapefruit juice	(none needed)
1 cup lemongrass stalks, plus ½ cup shredded coconut	4½ cups water	4 tablespoons lemon juice
1 cup rose-scented geranium leaves	2 cups boiling water and 2½ cups apple or white grape juice	4 tablespoons lemon juice
1 cup rosemary leaves, plus 2 cinnamon sticks and 6 whole cloves	4½ cups cranberry juice	(none needed)
¼ cup lemon verbena leaves	4½ cups water	4 tablespoons lemon juice

Hot Pepper Jelly

YIELD: 6 CUPS

A mixture of green, orange, and red sweet peppers is especially pretty. Make the jelly as hot as you like it by adding more or using fewer jalapeños. If you prefer a jelly with chunks of fruit in it, return a cup of the chopped peppers to the jelly after measuring the infusion. Use this jelly as a baste when you grill chicken. Or make the old-fashioned appetizer Jezebel Sauce: warm Hot Pepper Jelly and pour it over cream cheese; serve with celery-stick dippers.

3–4 sweet peppers, seeded and coarsely chopped
2–4 jalapeño peppers, seeded and coarsely chopped
2 cups boiling water
2½ cups (approximately) unsweetened apple juice or water
3½ cups granulated sugar
1 package Sure-Gel or other low-sugar pectin
4 tablespoons cider vinegar

1. Prepare six half-pint or three one-pint jars and lids as described for herb jelly on page 19.
2. Place sweet and jalapeño peppers in a saucepan with the boiling water and infuse for 1 hour.
3. Strain. (Reserve the chopped peppers if you plan to add them back into the jelly.) Measure the infusion and pour it into a large saucepan. Add enough apple juice or water to make 4½ cups total liquid. Stir in 1 cup of the reserved chopped peppers, if desired.
4. In a small bowl, mix ¼ cup of the sugar with the pectin. Whisk the mixture into the herb infusion.
5. Bring the infusion to a rolling boil. Stir in the remaining sugar and return to a boil. Boil hard for 1 full minute. Remove from the heat.
6. Skim off the foam. Stir in the vinegar.
7. Pour the jelly into the prepared jars, cover with sterile lids, and secure with ring. Can in hot water bath as described on page 19.

Rosemary-Goldenrod Jelly

Capture the golden sun of autumn with Goldenrod Jelly. This yields a fragrant sparkling jelly that makes everyone smile. In flower language, goldenrod connects you to the heavens. Infuse 2 cups of packed fresh goldenrod (*Solidago* species) flowers, then follow the herb jelly directions on page 20. Infuse several sprigs of fresh rosemary in the hot jelly before bottling.

Herb Honeys

Herb honeys are a snap to make. You can brew a batch with dried herbs any time of year. You'll also need unpasteurized honey, available from health-food stores or a local beekeeper. Choose the milder, light-colored honeys to give the herb flavor top billing. For herb flavorings, cinnamon basil leaves and flowering tops, lavender buds, rosemary leaves, chamomile flowers, rose-scented geranium leaves and flowers, and fragrant dianthus (carnations or clove pinks) flowers are my favorites.

Try this method with any herb combinations that appeal to you. The only rule is that you must use dried plant material because excess water from fresh herbs could dilute the honey enough to promote the growth of bacteria.

Use herb honeys in any recipe calling for honey and, of course, to sweeten herb tea. For a sweet spread for biscuits, whip a little herb honey into softened butter.

Safety first: *Use unsprayed herbs and flowers only!*

¼ cup dried herbs
1 cup honey

1. Place the dried herbs in a sterilized glass jar. Cover with honey. Cap the jar tightly and let it sit in a cool, dark place for two weeks.
2. Strain the honey through a sieve and rebottle it. (If the honey is thick, heat it slightly in a pan of hot water to make straining easier.)

CHAPTER 2

SPRING
Recipes

Infant seedlings rouse to the warming rays of the sun. Hopeful patches of chervil and cilantro appear, eager green shoots of fragrant mint push through the surface of the mellow earth, chickweed billows over the cold frame, and here and there dandelions and violets unfurl their blooms. It's spring! Every breath of new life is cause for rejoicing — at least for now.

We never say spring is on time; it's either early or late. Technically, spring begins on the vernal equinox. For me, spring is official with the first salad of tender lettuce garnished with chervil and strewn with violet blossoms, served with surprisingly meaty Dandy Burgers (page 30) made from — you guessed it — dandelion blossoms!

Rosemary Lima Bean Spread

SERVES 6-8

Astaple from the Mediterranean region, hummus consists of ground chickpeas combined with sesame paste. This lighter version is delicious spread on garlic toast or scooped up with roasted carrots or steamed broccoli and cauliflower. It also makes a good protein spread for a salad sandwich dressed with vinaigrette, or wrap the puree into lettuce leaves and top with chopped olives. I generally use equal amounts of lemon juice and Opal Basil-Garlic-Black Peppercorn Vinegar (page 118).

3 tablespoons olive oil
5–6 cloves garlic
1 tablespoon finely minced fresh rosemary
2 cups cooked lima beans
2 tablespoons lemon juice or herb vinegar

A few drops hot pepper oil or Tabasco sauce
Freshly ground black pepper, to taste
Finely minced fresh Italian parsley, for garnish

1. Heat 1 tablespoon of the olive oil in a small saucepan over medium-low heat. Sauté the garlic until it begins to turn golden. Stir in the rosemary and remove from the heat.
2. Place garlic, remaining olive oil, beans, lemon juice or vinegar, hot seasoning, and pepper in a food processor; process until smooth.
3. Pour into a serving bowl. Garnish with minced parsley and pepper.

A Wild Harvest

In early spring, use wild greens like dandelions *(Taraxacum officinale)*, chickweed *(Stellaria media)*, violets *(Viola papilionacea)*, watercress *(Nasturtium officinale)*, stinging nettles *(Urtica dioica)*, and chicory *(Cichorium intybus)*. Chop them fine and add a small handful to soup or a fresh green salad. Eat only unsprayed plants that you can positively identify.

Roasted Asparagus with Chervil and Violets

SERVES 4–6

When I first heard mention of roasted asparagus, I was aghast. Frizzle fresh asparagus? I tried it, though — delicious! This is easy, elegant appetizer fare, served hot or cold. For this recipe, thick asparagus stalks work best.

1 pound asparagus stalks, trimmed
2 tablespoons olive oil
Coarse sea salt
Lemon juice
Fresh chervil and violet blossoms, minced, for garnish

1. Preheat oven to 450°F.
2. Place the asparagus in a heavy roasting pan, or spread it on a baking sheet. Drizzle the olive oil over the asparagus, then turn to coat. Sprinkle lightly with salt. Bake 10 to 15 minutes, or until asparagus is soft.
3. To serve, arrange asparagus on a platter, squeeze a little lemon juice over it, and garnish with minced chervil and violet blossoms.

Edible Spring Flowers

Tulips are edible and tasty, too — just ask the deer, which can eliminate an entire tulip bed in one meal, much to a gardener's dismay! Separate the petals from a few flowers and dab them with egg salad for an appetizer or with lemon curd for dessert. Other tasty spring herb flowers include pansies, chives, carnations, lavender, roses, thyme, borage, bergamot, dandelions, sweet woodruff, elderflowers, and calendulas. Eat only unsprayed posies that you can positively identify. Avoid blossoms from the florist, which most likely have been sprayed.

Lavender and rose petals

Slimming Miso Soup

SERVES 4

Miso soup is one of the gentlest ways to transition your body from traditionally heavy winter foods to lighter spring fare. And if like me at this time of the year you want to shed a few pounds before even considering a bathing suit, miso soup makes a nourishing, satisfying meal, whether for breakfast, lunch, or dinner. Miso soup is also an excellent choice for anyone convalescing from illness.

1 package (8.8 ounces) soba noodles

1 tablespoon raw sesame seeds

1 teaspoon roasted sesame oil

2 medium carrots, cut into ⅛-inch rounds

1 tablespoon grated raw gingerroot

⅓ cup thinly sliced shiitake mushrooms

6 cups water (use the drained cooking water from the noodles)

1 strip (3 inches) kombu seaweed, cut into slivers

6 scallions, slivered, with a little of the green

1 cup diced tofu

½ cup barley miso (available at natural food stores)

½ cup minced garlic chives

1. Cook the noodles according to package directions. Drain, reserving 6 cups of the cooking water.
2. Dry-toast the sesame seeds in a small, cast-iron skillet over low heat until fragrant. Reserve.
3. Heat the sesame oil in a large saucepan over medium heat. Sauté the carrots for 1 to 2 minutes, then stir in the gingerroot and mushrooms, and sauté 1 minute longer.
4. Add the water and seaweed. Stir. Bring the soup to a boil and adjust the heat to simmering. Cover, then cook for 10 minutes, or until the carrots are tender but not mushy.
5. Remove 1 cup of the broth and place in a small bowl. Add the scallions and tofu to the soup so they will warm through.

6. Stir the miso into the small bowl of broth, then combine the miso mixture with the soup.

7. Fill each bowl half full with noodles. Sprinkle the noodles with the garlic chives. Ladle the hot soup over the noodles and chives. Garnish with sesame seeds and serve immediately.

Lettuce and Lovage Soup

SERVES 4

On a cool spring evening, a quick soup makes a satisfying meal, especially when served with fresh warm bread or biscuits, topped with parsley and chive or tarragon herb butter (see page 13).

5 cups chicken or vegetable stock

2 red potatoes, scrubbed (but not peeled) and grated

1 medium leek, white and tender green parts only, cut into thin rounds

1 head leaf lettuce, shredded

½ cup chopped lovage (leaves and stems)

¼ cup chopped fresh flat-leaf parsley

1 tablespoon chopped fresh mint

1 tablespoon chopped fresh dill

1 tablespoon chopped fresh tarragon

Salt and freshly ground black pepper, to taste

Herb butter (see page 13)

Calendula petals, for garnish (optional)

Parsley

1. In a large pot, heat the chicken or vegetable stock to boiling. Add the potatoes, leek, and lettuce, and cook for 10 minutes over medium heat or until the vegetables are soft.

2. Stir in the chopped herbs. Cover the pot, remove from heat, and let sit for 5 minutes.

3. Return the soup to a simmer. Season with salt and pepper, and serve immediately with a dab of herb butter and calendula petals.

Cilantro Pesto Pizza

SERVES 2 (4 MEDIUM-SIZE PIECES)

Here's a great way to use the cilantro before it bolts. Pesto is a sauce made with an herb (usually basil) and garlic, oil, nuts, and cheese. This cilantro pesto tops a pizza. Serve with a salad for a light repast, or cut the pizza into small pieces for appetizers.

2 cups packed fresh cilantro (leaves and tender stems)
1–2 coarsely chopped jalapeño peppers
3–4 cloves garlic, finely minced
½ teaspoon salt
¼ cup fruity extra-virgin olive oil
¼ cup ricotta cheese
1 unbaked pizza shell (10 inches)
Freshly ground black pepper
½ cup grated Parmesan or pecorino cheese
1 cup grated mozzarella cheese

1. Preheat oven to 425°F.
2. Place the cilantro, peppers, garlic, and salt in a food processor. Process until evenly ground. With the motor running, pour in the olive oil in a thin stream. Process until pureed. Add the ricotta cheese and process just until blended.
3. Spread the pesto on the pizza shell. Add a few grinds of pepper, then spread the Parmesan or pecorino and the mozzarella on top.
4. Bake for 12 to 15 minutes, or until bubbly and golden. Serve immediately.

Pasta with Cilantro Pesto

Cilantro pesto is also wonderful over pasta: Thin the herb/pepper/garlic puree above with enough extra-virgin olive oil to make a sauce. Or, to reduce calories, use some of the pasta cooking water and less oil to thin the puree.

Traditional Mint Tabbouleh

SERVES 8

Taking the care to mince the ingredients extra-fine distributes the flavors so perfectly in this recipe that the extra effort really does make a big difference. Taste the tabbouleh before adding salt — the lemon juice may replace the need for it. Tabbouleh keeps well, covered, in the refrigerator for five days.

1 cup uncooked bulgur	1 large cucumber, peeled, seeded,
2 cups boiling water or	and finely diced
vegetable stock	2 plum tomatoes, peeled and diced
Juice of 4 lemons	⅓ cup fruity extra-virgin olive oil
½ cup finely minced fresh	1 teaspoon freshly ground black
flat-leaf parsley	pepper
½ cup finely minced fresh	Salt
mint	Finely minced fresh mint, for
8 scallions, finely chopped	garnish

1. Rinse and drain the bulgur and place it in a large bowl. Pour the boiling water or vegetable stock over the bulgur and cover with a plate or tea towel. Let sit until all the liquid is absorbed — about 15 minutes.
2. Toss the remaining ingredients except for the mint garnish with the bulgur.
3. Chill before serving. Garnish with the fresh mint.

Crazy for Calamint

Calamint *(Calamintha nepeta)* has small leaves with a distinctive spicy flavor, somewhat like spearmint but with more bite. In Italy, where the plant grows wild (it's called nepitella there), chefs use it to season mushrooms and potatoes. The flavor is wonderful in tabbouleh, as well as in Spring Flower Scones (page 38). The plant itself is a joy — drought-resistant, deer-proof, and trembling with bees and butterflies.

Dandy Burgers

SERVES 2 (4 MEDIUM-SIZE BURGERS)

Although some see dandelions as irritating weeds rather than sunny blossoms lighting up their lawns, anyone can enjoy dandelion burgers. Believe it or not, these tasty patties remind me of crab cakes, especially when served with cocktail sauce. Come on, give it a try. (Of course, never eat anything from a lawn that has been sprayed with chemicals.)

2 cups packed freshly opened dandelion blossoms
1 cup crumbled saltine or Ritz crackers
½ cup finely chopped onion
2 tablespoons Dijon mustard
2 tablespoons finely minced flat-leaved parsley
Dash Tabasco sauce
Salt and freshly ground black pepper, to taste
1 egg, well beaten
1 tablespoon safflower oil or butter, for frying
Cocktail sauce (optional)

Dandelion

1. To prepare the dandelion flowers, trim off all the bitter green stems with scissors. Cut the blossoms into quarters. Mix the trimmed blossoms with the remaining ingredients, except cocktail sauce.

2. Shape into patties.

3. Fry over medium heat until golden brown on both sides, about 8 minutes in total. Serve hot, with cocktail sauce if desired.

Watercress Salad with Citrus Dressing

SERVES 4

This is a refreshing spring salad for a low-calorie, high-energy lunch. By the way, if you have a good source for watercress, try making watercress pesto. Follow the recipe for Basil-Parsley Pesto on page 58, substituting 4 cups of fresh watercress for the basil and parsley. Watercress makes an excellent substitute for basil pesto, months before you can enjoy that treat from the garden.

1 tablespoon chopped walnuts

1 bunch watercress, torn into small pieces

2 hard-cooked eggs, sliced

3 tablespoons fresh orange juice

2 tablespoons fresh lemon juice

1 teaspoon roasted sesame oil

⅓ cup walnut oil

Freshly ground black pepper, to taste

2 tablespoons finely minced fresh chervil or cilantro

1. Dry-toast the walnuts in a small cast-iron skillet. Reserve.
2. Place the watercress on individual salad plates, and arrange the egg slices on top.
3. Whisk the juices and oils in a small bowl. Drizzle over the salad.
4. Add pepper, and garnish with the minced chervil or cilantro.

Floral Salad Plates

Try this special presentation for Mother's Day or any special spring celebration. You'll need two salad plates for each serving — they'll be stacked on top of each other. The top plate should be a little smaller and must be glass or crystal; the bottom plate can be glass or a solid color. On the larger bottom plate, arrange a pretty pattern of green leaves and colorful flowers, such as dill, pansies, flat-leaved parsley, chives, carnations, and bergamot. For the top plate, prepare your favorite mixed-green salad. Set the plate of salad over the larger plate. As the salad is eaten, the flower plate will be revealed!

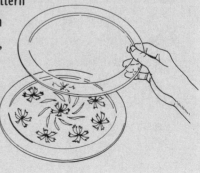

Pasta with Field Greens and Basil-Peanut Sauce

SERVES 4–6

Fragrant and rich, this dish is perfect for a day when you've expended many calories digging in the herb garden! Before heading toward the kitchen, cut field greens like dandelions, chicory, and cress, or garden vegetables like bok choy, collards, mizuna, endive, watercress, and arugula. (Don't cook the watercress or arugula — they'll wilt enough when tossed with hot noodles and sauce.) Any leftover sauce makes wonderful dressing for a salad of watercress, sliced chicken, oranges, snow peas, and scallions.

For the Basil–Peanut Sauce
1½ cups unsalted roasted peanuts
2–3 cloves garlic, finely minced
  1-inch slice fresh gingerroot, cut
  into chunks
2 tablespoons tamari or soy sauce
1 teaspoon roasted sesame oil
1 scant tablespoon frozen basil
  puree (see page 116), or
  2 tablespoons fresh basil
Pinch of cayenne pepper
Juice of 1 lime
1 tablespoon orange juice
  concentrate

For the Pasta
1 pound linguine
1 tablespoon herb vinegar,
  such as Opal Basil-Garlic-
  Black Peppercorn (page
  118) or nasturtium flower
  vinegar
2 cups julienned mixed
  field greens
½ cup scallions, cut into
  small rounds

1. Place all the Basil-Peanut Sauce ingredients in a food processor. Process until almost smooth — a few chunks are nice.
2. Meanwhile, cook pasta according to package directions, adding a tablespoon of herb vinegar to the cooking water. Add the julienned greens to the boiling pasta about 2 minutes before the pasta is done.
3. Allow the water to return to a boil, cook for 1 minute, then drain, reserving about ½ cup of the water to thin the sauce.
4. Dress the hot pasta with the peanut sauce and scallions, adding some of the reserved cooking water if needed.

Lemon Herb Rice

SERVES 6–8

This fragrant rice blend is an ideal match for Oriental-style stir-fries and fish dishes. Feel free to use a rice cooker to prepare the rice; it makes perfect rice every time with no fuss.

2 cups jasmine rice	1 tablespoon dried mint
3 cups stock or water	1 teaspoon dried lemon verbena
3 stalks lemongrass	1/8 teaspoon ground cumin
2–3 garlic cloves, finely minced	1 teaspoon lemon zest
1 tablespoon butter	Pinch of cayenne pepper

1. Wash and drain the rice. Place rice, stock or water, lemongrass, garlic, and butter in a medium-size saucepan. Bring to a boil, lower heat to simmering, and place the cover slightly askew so steam can vent. Cook until water is absorbed, 10 to 15 minutes. Remove from heat, close lid tightly, and let steam 10 to 15 minutes more.
2. Grind the dried herbs and the lemon zest finely.
3. Open the saucepan and discard lemongrass stalks. Toss the rice with the ground herbs, lemon zest, and cayenne. Serve immediately.

May Day

Once upon a time, I beheaded my mother's spring garden to make May baskets for the neighbors. Even though I made one for her, Mom was not amused. To avoid this catastrophe in your yard, help your children create construction paper cones strewn with ribbons and filled with fragrant bundles of herbs (such as *bouquet garni* on page 10) and violets (or whatever you have plenty of). The fun is to get up early in the morning, hang the basket on a neighbor's door knob, ring the doorbell, and run away as fast as your little legs will carry you!

Roasted Scallions

SERVES 4–6

Serve this delicious side dish with meats, chicken, or grilled fish. If you're grilling, toss scallions with oil and put them on the grill during the last 3 to 5 minutes of cooking the entree. Turn once.

> 24 scallions
> Extra-virgin olive oil
> Juice of 1 lemon
> Salt and freshly ground black pepper, to taste
> Finely minced chervil, parsley, or cilantro, for garnish

1. Preheat oven to 475°F.
2. Trim the root end and the tough part of the green stalks from the scallions. Arrange the scallions in a single layer on a baking sheet. Drizzle them lightly with olive oil, turning to coat evenly.
3. Roast scallions 15 to 20 minutes, turning once or twice, until they are tender and lightly browned. Remove them from the oven.
4. Arrange scallions on a serving dish and sprinkle with lemon juice. Season with salt and pepper. Garnish with freshly minced herbs.

Herb-Dyed Easter Eggs

Natural-dyed eggs are beautiful in baskets and table arrangements. Fill a large saucepan with leaves or vegetable skins (see below). Cover with water, and boil for 10 minutes. Add the eggs and boil 5 minutes more. Remove from heat and cover the pot until cool. If you plan to eat the eggs, refrigerate them as soon as they're cool. If you are using them only for decoration, you can let them sit in the dye water for several hours or overnight. **Herbs to Try:** Sage or nettle greens for khaki brown; dandelion blossoms for bright yellow; ground turmeric (2 teaspoons per cup water) for gold; onion skins for mahogany; red cabbage leaves plus 1 tablespoon vinegar for purplish blue; red beets plus 1 tablespoon vinegar for pink.

Shrimp Cakes with Cilantro Mint Chutney

SERVES 4 (MAKES 8 SMALL CAKES)

Here's a nice change from fish cakes that creates a company meal in minutes. Serve with Roasted Asparagus (page 25) or sautéed snow peas, and a fresh green salad.

For the Shrimp Cakes

- 1 pound cooked shrimp, chopped
- 1 celery stalk, finely minced
- 5 scallions, white part only, cut into small rounds
- ½ cup crushed Ritz or saltine crackers
- 2 tablespoons finely minced fresh parsley
- 2 tablespoons finely minced fresh chervil or cilantro
- Pinch of cayenne pepper
- 1 egg, well beaten
- 1 tablespoon unsalted butter for frying

For the Chutney

- ½ tablespoon unsalted butter
- 2 cloves garlic, finely minced
- ⅓ cup slivered almonds
- 1 cup packed spearmint leaves
- 1 cup packed cilantro leaves
- 2 tablespoons plain low-fat yogurt
- 1 tablespoon lime juice
- 2 teaspoons herb jelly or honey
- Salt and freshly ground black pepper, to taste

1. Combine the shrimp, celery, scallions, crackers, parsley, chervil or cilantro, cayenne, and egg in a medium-size bowl. Refrigerate for 1 hour before frying.

2. In the meantime, make the chutney. Heat ½ tablespoon of butter in a small saucepan over medium-low heat. Sauté the garlic and almonds until golden brown.

3. Place the garlic and almonds in a food processor, and process until the almonds are ground. Add the remaining ingredients and process until well combined. Let mixture cool to room temperature.

4. Heat 1 tablespoon of butter or oil in a large sauté pan. Form eight small cakes from the shrimp mixture, and brown them on both sides. Serve hot, with the chutney at room temperature.

Poached Salmon with Dill Yogurt Sauce

An easy, festive dish that's delicious hot or cold. Serve it with Roasted Vegetable Treats (page 63) and a fresh green salad for a simple-to-make company meal. Here's an opportunity to use nasturtium capers if you pickled some last summer (see page 122).

For the Dill Yogurt Sauce
- 1 tablespoon unsalted butter
- 2 shallots, finely minced
- 2 tablespoons finely chopped fresh dill
- 1 tablespoon finely chopped fresh chervil
- 1 tablespoon capers
- 1 teaspoon fresh lemon juice
- 1/8 teaspoon white pepper
- 1 cup plain nonfat yogurt

For the Poached Salmon
- 6 cups water
- 2 cups unsweetened apple or white grape juice
- 6 stalks lemongrass
- 2 cloves garlic, peeled and halved
- 1/2 cup sliced scallions
- 1/2 cup fresh parsley
- 2 bay leaves
- 2 pounds thick salmon fillets, cut into four equal pieces

1. For the Dill Yogurt Sauce, heat butter in small saucepan over medium-low heat. Sauté the shallots until they are golden brown. Remove pan from the heat.

2. Combine the butter and shallots with the remaining ingredients in a small bowl. Heat until warm (do not boil) if serving with hot fish, or chill for use with cold fish.

3. Place the water, apple or grape juice, lemongrass, garlic, scallions, parsley, and bay leaves in a large saucepan or fish poacher. Bring to a boil, then reduce heat and simmer for 10 minutes.

4. Slide the salmon into the hot liquid. Adjust heat until there is a slight ripple of water bubbling over the fish. Cover. Cook 8 to 10 minutes.

5. Carefully remove the salmon from the pan and arrange it on a platter. Serve hot or chilled with Dill Yogurt Sauce.

Dill

Uncle Bicky's Not-Red Barbecued Chicken

SERVES 6–8

When the first warm weekend rolls into town, it's time to make iced tea and fire up the grill for the best barbecued chicken you've ever eaten. This is not your sticky-sweet red barbecue sauce, but a tangy concoction as flavorful as my Eastern Shore kin. It's delicious hot or cold.

¼ cup kosher salt
1 teaspoon freshly ground black pepper
3 tablespoons Poultry Seasoning (page 11)
1½ cups apple cider vinegar
1 egg
2 fryer chickens, cut into pieces

1. Place the salt and pepper, Poultry Seasoning, vinegar, and egg in a blender, and whiz for 30 seconds or until well combined.
2. Place the chicken pieces in zipper-lock plastic bags or a large bowl and cover with sauce, reserving ¼ cup for basting. Marinate in the refrigerator for several hours, turning occasionally to coat evenly.
3. Grill chicken pieces until they're done, about 20 to 45 minutes, depending on size of chicken pieces and amount of heat in coals. Baste with reserved marinade for the first 5 minutes of cooking.

An Herbal Basting Brush

A branch of rosemary or sage makes a flavorful (and compostable!) brush for basting vegetables and meats on the grill. Bundle several together, mixing "flavors" if you wish, and tie them with raffia. Give one as a gift, with one of your favorite grilling recipes and a jar of savory herb jelly tucked into the package.

Spring Flower Scones

MAKES ABOUT 10 SCONES

Edible flowers are all the rage, but not many people explore the possibilities beyond garnishing a salad. Here's your chance. Gather a handful of fresh bergamot, calendula, 'Lemon Gem' marigolds, nasturtiums, dianthus, borage, thyme, calamint, sweet woodruff, or chive blooms. Feel free to combine, tasting as you go along. Most of all, have fun! Needless to say, these scones are even more delicious served with herb jelly.

> 2 cups unbleached white flour
> 2 teaspoons baking soda
> ¼ cup sugar
> ½ teaspoon salt
> ¼ cup unsalted butter, cut into bits
> ½ cup currants or golden raisins
> 1 teaspoon orange zest
> ¼ cup fresh flower petals, torn into small pieces
> ⅓ cup sour milk or buttermilk
> 2 eggs
> 1 teaspoon vanilla

1. Preheat the oven to 450°F.
2. Mix the flour, baking soda, sugar, and salt in a medium-size bowl.
3. Cut the butter into the flour mixture with a fork or pastry cutter.
4. Mix in the currants or raisins, orange zest, and flower petals.
5. Beat the milk, eggs, and vanilla in a small bowl.
6. Make a well in the center of the dry ingredients, and pour in the milk-egg mixture; mix until just combined.
7. Roll out dough on a floured board and cut with a biscuit cutter, or drop the dough by large spoonfuls (about ¼ cup) onto a greased baking sheet.
8. Bake for 12 to 15 minutes, or until golden brown.

Lavender Lemon Bars

MAKES ABOUT 28 SQUARES

These old-fashioned delights never fail to please, and often appear at wedding and baby showers. They freeze well, so you can make them ahead of time for a special event. For a special touch, frame the serving tray by scattering fresh lavender sprigs around the bars.

¾ cup butter
½ cup confectioners' sugar
2 cups flour
½ cup ground slivered almonds
2 teaspoons lemon zest
2 teaspoons lavender buds
4 eggs
1¾ cups granulated sugar
⅓ cup flour
⅓ cup lemon juice
½ teaspoon baking soda
Confectioners' sugar and a few ground lavender buds, for garnish

1. Preheat the oven to 350°F.
2. Cream the butter and confectioners' sugar in a medium-size bowl until well-blended.
3. Add the flour, almonds, lemon zest, and lavender. Mix by hand until well combined.
4. Pat the dough evenly into a lightly greased 9 × 13-inch baking pan.
5. Bake for 20 minutes. Leave the oven on. Remove pan from the oven and cool slightly.
6. Beat the eggs and sugar in a small bowl. Whisk in the remaining ingredients, and beat until well blended. Pour over the crust.
7. Return the pan to the oven and bake 25 minutes, or until golden brown. Cool.
8. Sprinkle with a little confectioners' sugar and a few ground lavender buds. Cut into squares.

Slimming Spring Teas

Each of these recipes makes a large pot of hot tea, enough for two or three servings. Follow the directions on page 17 for a Perfect Pot of Herb Tea. For the most delicate flavor, allow the tea to steep for 8 to 10 minutes. For stronger flavor (and more vitamins and minerals), let it stand 30 minutes. When serving tea, it's fun to place a fresh (edible!) flower blossom such as a violet, carnation, or rosebud in the bottom of the cup before pouring the tea.

For the Flower Power blend, be sure to identify the elderflower positively. The edible varieties have bluish black or purplish black berries; avoid the red-berried kinds. To be on the safe side, dry elderflowers before using them for tea. All parts of fresh elderberry can cause allergic reactions. You can purchase dried elderflowers from herb suppliers and health-food stores.

Thinny Mint
>   1 large handful fresh chickweed *(Stellaria media)*
>   8 sprigs spearmint leaves
>   8 violet flowers
>   3 cups boiling water

Green Balm
>   8 tops tender fresh stinging nettle *(Urtica dioica)*
>   8 sprigs fresh lemon balm leaves
>   4 sprigs peppermint
>   3 cups boiling water

Flower Power
>   4 sprigs fresh lavender buds
>   4 chamomile flowering tops
>   1 tablespoon dried elderflowers *(Sambucus canadensis)*
>   2 sprigs anise hyssop leaves
>   3 cups boiling water

CHAPTER 3

SUMMER

Recipes

ummer menus sing a lighthearted song of
sweet basil and tomatoes, and fresh summer
vegetables and fruits need little fancy fixing.
Who wants to stay in the kitchen anyway? Enjoy
these seasonal foods enhanced with cooling herbs like
basil, marjoram, dill, and savory or, alternatively, pumped so
high with hot chilies that sweltering August temperatures
feel cool by comparison. Even if you don't have a garden,
farm stands provide abundant harvests, so fill your gathering
basket and support your local growers. We've waited all year,
and summer is finally here!

Broiled Pesto Vegetable Rounds

SERVES 6–8 AS APPETIZERS

Leftover pesto or frozen herb paste (see page 116) makes this quick appetizer especially easy to make. I like to arrange three whole pumpkin seeds on each vegetable round. The pesto is also good spread on baguette slices and broiled for quick toasts to serve as appetizers with soup. Any leftover pesto will keep in the refrigerator for at least two weeks. Pour a thin film of olive oil over the pesto to prevent discoloration.

For the Pesto
- ¼ cup packed fresh summer savory leaves
- ¾ cup fresh Italian parsley leaves
- 2 tablespoons extra-virgin olive oil
- 1–2 minced garlic cloves
- 1 tablespoon lemon juice
- Pinch of salt

For the Vegetables
- 12 new potatoes, scrubbed and cut in half
- 2 summer squash, cut in ¼-inch rounds
- ⅓–½ cup pumpkin seeds, walnuts, sunflower seeds, or pine nuts, for topping
- Parmesan cheese
- Freshly ground black pepper, to taste

1. Chop the herbs in a food processor or blender. With the motor running, pour in the olive oil in a thin stream. Add the remaining pesto ingredients and blend until smooth. Set aside.
2. Steam potatoes for 5 minutes to partially cook them.
3. Set the broiler rack 6 inches from the source of heat, and turn on the broiler.
4. Cover a cookie sheet with aluminum foil and spray it with non-stick cooking spray.
5. Lay the vegetables in a single layer on the cookie sheet. Use a tablespoon to spread them with a thin coating of pesto. Arrange the seeds or nuts on top, and finish with a sprinkle of Parmesan cheese.
6. Broil until the topping is sizzling, about 3 to 5 minutes. Season with pepper to taste, and serve immediately.

Roasted Green Beans

SERVES 4–6

Roasted green beans make an easy but fancy side dish with fish or chicken entrees. And they are also great as an appetizer when green beans from the summer garden are bountiful.

2 tablespoons olive oil
1 pound fresh whole green beans, trimmed
10–12 medium cloves garlic, peeled and thinly sliced
1 cup slivered almonds
2 tablespoons minced fresh rosemary
1 tablespoon tamari or soy sauce
2 tablespoons Opal Basil-Garlic-Black Peppercorn Vinegar (page 118)
Freshly ground black pepper

1. Preheat the oven to 425°F. Spray a baking sheet with nonstick cooking spray.
2. Spread the green beans on the baking sheet. Sprinkle with olive oil, garlic, almonds, rosemary, and tamari or soy sauce. Turn to coat.
3. Bake 20 minutes, shaking the tray occasionally to encourage even baking.
4. Transfer the beans to a serving dish. Drizzle with the vinegar and season with pepper. Serve warm.

Orange and Red Tomato Salsa with Cilantro

MAKES 2–3 CUPS

American taste is changing: Salsa now outsells ketchup! This is a basic recipe — you can add diced tomatillos, sweet peppers, and/or cucumbers. The sweeter flavor of orange tomatoes adds a delicious and colorful touch, but don't worry if you can't find any. Meaty Italian tomatoes like Romas make a thicker salsa. If your tomatoes are juicy, strain out some of the liquid before adding the remaining ingredients. Out of cilantro? Use chopped basil or other salsa herbs (see below). Serve salsa as a dip with chips or as a topping for burgers, fajitas, or open-faced grilled cheese sandwiches. Salsa is also delicious on pizza.

1 red tomato, skinned and cubed

1 orange tomato, skinned and cubed

2 tablespoons finely minced red or Vidalia onion

½ cup finely minced fresh cilantro, plus extra for garnish

1 tablespoon fresh lime juice

1 tablespoon finely minced jalapeño pepper (dragon-breath types can use more!)

1. Mix together all ingredients in a small bowl. Use immediately, or refrigerate until serving time.
2. To serve, garnish with additional cilantro if desired.

Other Salsa Herbs

When hot summertime weather hits, cilantro withers. Try growing papalo (*Porophyllum ruderale* spp. *macrocephalum*) from Mexico and quillquina (*Porophyllum ruderale*) from Bolivia, two salsa herbs that can really take the heat. Both of these herbs have stronger flavors than that of cilantro, so use half as much as a recipe calls for, and taste before adding more.

Watermelon and Honeydew Salsa with Spearmint

MAKES 4 CUPS

Great with broiled fish or chicken, this salsa tastes best if used within a few hours. To vary the recipe, substitute chocolate mint or cinnamon basil for a sweeter flavor, or use cilantro for a Mexican touch.

> 2 cups chopped and seeded watermelon
>
> 2 cups chopped and seeded honeydew melon
>
> ¼ cup finely minced red or Vidalia onion
>
> 2 tablespoons finely minced jalapeño pepper
>
> 2 tablespoons finely chopped fresh spearmint
>
> Juice of 2 lemons or limes
>
> 1 teaspoon sugar or maple syrup

Combine ingredients in a large bowl. Cover and refrigerate for 1 hour before serving.

Mango Salsa

MAKES 3 CUPS

A somewhat mellow salsa, mango cools dishes like spicy stir-fries and curry. It's also good with grilled chicken or turkey wraps. Try this same recipe with peaches or cantaloupe instead of mango.

> 2 cups diced ripe mango
>
> 1 cucumber, peeled, seeded, and diced
>
> 1 clove garlic, finely minced
>
> ¼ cup finely minced red or Vidalia onion
>
> 1 tablespoon finely minced jalapeño pepper
>
> 2 tablespoons finely minced fresh basil
>
> 1 teaspoon brown sugar
>
> 2 tablespoons lime juice
>
> Pinch of sea salt

Combine ingredients in a small bowl. Cover and refrigerate 2 to 3 hours before serving.

Cantaloupe Buttermilk Soup
Laced with Wasabi and Raspberry Swirls

SERVES 4–6

This cold soup is a special treat when luscious ripe cantaloupes roll into the market. It's ready to serve in minutes, yet tastes like you've spent hours perfecting the flavors. Wasabi is a Japanese horseradish-like condiment, typically served with sushi. It's available from Asian specialty and gourmet stores in both powdered and paste form. If you can't find it, substitute horseradish.

> 1 medium-size cantaloupe
> 1 tablespoon orange juice concentrate
> 1½ cups buttermilk, plus additional buttermilk for sauce
> 2 tablespoons raspberry preserves
> 1 tablespoon wasabi paste
> Red bergamot and calendula blossoms, for garnish

1. Puree the first three ingredients in a blender. Chill.
2. When ready to serve, mix the raspberry preserves with enough buttermilk to make a thin sauce. In a separate dish, do the same with the wasabi.
3. Spoon the cantaloupe puree into serving bowls. Swirl a little raspberry sauce into each bowl. Repeat with the wasabi sauce.
4. Decorate each bowl with the calendula and bergamot petals.

Pretty as a Picture

Many garden flowers and most herb blossoms make delightful edible garnishes. Safe and tasty choices include begonia, bergamot, borage, calendula, carnation, scented geraniums, hollyhocks, honeysuckle, 'Lemon Gem' marigolds, Mexican marigolds, nasturtiums, portulaca, rosemary, roses, scarlet runner bean, snapdragon, thyme, and yucca. Use small whole blossoms or petals from larger flowers. Use only unsprayed plants (not from florists).

Tomato Tarragon Soup

MAKES ABOUT 2 QUARTS

An easy, elegant dish, Tomato Tarragon Soup can be made even prettier if you ladle it into individual bowls and swirl in a little plain yogurt thinned with a teaspoon of tarragon vinegar. Garnish with a few leaves of fresh tarragon and calendula petals. See Pretty as a Picture on page 46 for additional ideas for fresh flower garnishes. If there's no fresh gingerroot on hand, substitute 1 teaspoon powdered ginger when adding the tarragon. Black-Skillet Corn Bread (page 59) is a nice complement to this dish.

2 tablespoons extra-virgin olive oil

1 tablespoon butter

1 cup diced shallots

1 tablespoon grated fresh gingerroot

5 pounds red ripe tomatoes, peeled and cut into large pieces

1 teaspoon salt

2 tablespoons fresh tarragon, minced

Salt and freshly ground black pepper, to taste

1. Heat the oil and butter in a large saucepan over medium-low heat. Add the shallots and gingerroot, and sauté for a few minutes until shallots soften.

2. Add the tomatoes and salt. Cover, bring to a boil, then lower heat and simmer gently for 1 hour. Check occasionally to make sure there is enough liquid.

3. Add the tarragon and cook for 20 minutes more.

4. Cool for 30 mintues. Puree in the blender. If desired, pass the puree through a food mill to remove seeds. Season with salt and pepper to taste. Serve hot or cold.

Tarragon

Pasta Salad with Field Greens

SERVES 2 FOR DINNER, 4 AS A SIDE DISH

When lettuce goes to seed, the gardener must find ingenious alternatives. Take a second look at what are commonly considered weeds. Mild-tasting lamb's-quarters are abundant in my garden and very nutritious to boot. You can substitute amaranth, dandelion, orach, or purslane. Don't tell finicky eaters that these are weeds, and they'll gobble them down. You may want to add vegetables like diced summer squash and thinly sliced bok choy to this recipe as well, dropping them into the boiling pasta a minute or two before tossing in the greens. I like the multicolored effect of the vegetables with bow-tie pasta for this dish, but any type of small, sturdy pasta will do.

1 pound pasta
2 cups coarsely chopped lamb's-quarters
3 tablespoons extra-virgin olive oil
1 tablespoon herb/red wine vinegar
½ cup minced fresh garlic chives
2 tablespoons minced fresh marjoram
¼–½ cup Parmesan cheese
Salt and freshly ground black pepper, to taste

1. Fill a large stockpot with salted water, and bring to a boil. Cook the pasta according to package directions.
2. Two minutes before the pasta is done, add the lamb's-quarters or other greens. When the water returns to a boil, begin timing for the last 2 minutes.
3. Pour the contents into a colander, and run cold water over them to cool slightly. Drain.
4. Pour into a serving bowl. Mix in the olive oil, vinegar, and herbs, and stir to combine well. Sprinkle with the Parmesan cheese, and season with salt and pepper to taste.

Lamb's-quarters

Favorite Summer Potherbs

Lamb's-quarters *(Chenopodium album)* are a common garden weed in the same family as beets. Harvest the tops of seedlings when they first appear. If plants are large — they grow quickly — trim the tender ends of side branches. Lamb's-quarters can double for spinach in any recipe, and actually contain more iron. Purslane *(Portulaca oleracea)* is a shiny-leaved, low-growing weed that pops up once the ground warms. Try it raw mixed with chopped tomatoes, olive oil, vinegar, and basil. Purslane is extremely high in the healthful omega-3 fatty acids for which fish is famous, and it tastes a lot better than fish oil!

Totally Herb Salad

SERVES 4

Salads just from herbs? Très gourmet. Serve small portions on beautiful plates garnished with herb blossoms (bergamot, borage, calendula, nasturtiums, or whatever you have available). I like to serve this after the main dish as a segue to dessert. Use a piquant dressing such as Autumn Walnut Vinaigrette (page 71) made with nasturtium blossom vinegar.

> 1 cup torn basil leaves
> ¼ cup minced marjoram leaves
> ¼ cup minced borage leaves
> ¼ cup finely minced parsley leaves
> ¼ cup minced garlic chives
> Freshly ground black pepper, to taste
> Herb blossoms, for garnish

1. Combine herb leaves and chives in a small bowl. Chill until serving time.
2. Dress and arrange on individual salad plates. Season with pepper and strew with the herb blossoms.

Green Beans with Garlic and Savory

SERVES 4

When green beans are abundant, steam enough for several meals, undercooking them slightly. At mealtime, stir-fry them in a nonstick skillet. Try this same recipe with fresh summer squash cut into small strips.

1 pound green beans, trimmed
1 tablespoon olive oil
2 cloves garlic, minced
1 tablespoon minced fresh savory, for garnish

1. Steam the green beans for 5 minutes. They should still be crisp. Refrigerate them until you're ready to serve.
2. Heat the olive oil in a skillet over medium-low heat. Sauté the garlic briefly until it begins to turn golden. Add the beans and toss until heated through. Serve garnished with the fresh savory.

Zucchini Fritters with Cheese and Basil

SERVES 4

An easy, satisfying meal for any time of day, these fritters are good with applesauce or Hot Pepper Jelly (page 21). Arrowhead Mills makes a terrific multigrain pancake mix; you may find it at your local natural-foods store.

1 pound zucchini, grated (about 3 cups)
¼ cup finely minced onion
¼ teaspoon salt
2 tablespoons finely minced fresh basil
¾ cup pancake mix
⅓ cup finely chopped walnuts
½ cup grated cheddar cheese
½ cup skim milk
1 large egg, well beaten
Scant tablespoon canola oil for the pan

1. Place the grated zucchini and the onion in a sieve. Sprinkle with the salt and let stand 10 minutes. Squeeze to extract excess liquid, then place in a medium-size bowl.
2. Combine the basil, pancake mix, walnuts, and grated cheese in a small bowl.
3. Combine the milk and beaten egg, and stir into the zucchini mixture. Add the pancake mixture and stir until just combined.
4. Heat a small amount of canola oil in a nonstick frying pan over medium heat. Fry fritters, turning once, until cooked through and golden brown on both sides.

Summer Pizza with Zucchini, Provolone, Feta, and Artichoke Hearts

MAKES 4 MEDIUM-SIZE PIECES

With ready-made flatbreads for the crust, this delicious dinner can be prepared in minutes. The flatbread I like best is made by Garden of Eatin. Flatbreads freeze well and are handy to have on reserve for emergency appetizers.

1 flatbread (8 x 11 inches)
¼ pound provolone cheese, thinly sliced
2 medium zucchini, cut lengthwise into very thin slices
1 cup canned artichoke hearts, drained and cut into small pieces
1 small Vidalia onion, finely sliced
1 tablespoon minced fresh marjoram
Freshly ground black pepper, to taste
½ cup crumbled feta cheese

1. Preheat the oven to 475°F. Spray a cookie sheet with nonstick cooking spray.
2. Place the flatbread on the cookie sheet. Cover the flatbread with the provolone cheese, then layer on the zucchini. Sprinkle with the artichokes, onion, marjoram, and pepper. Top with the feta cheese.
3. Bake for 8 to 10 minutes, or until golden brown.

Savory Corn Pancakes with Chicken Sausage

For a cool, outdoor dinner, set up your electric frying pan on the porch, and cook up these corn pancakes. If you're in a chopping mood, pair them with homemade chicken sausage, which is scrumptious and almost fat-free. You can substitute frozen corn, but fresh is always better! Leftover sausage is a terrific filling for sandwich wraps, served with Mango Salsa (page 45).

For the Chicken Sausage
- 1 pound boneless and skinless chicken breasts, diced
- ¾ tart apple, finely chopped
- ¼ cup onion, finely chopped
- 2 cloves garlic, finely chopped
- 1 teaspoon finely chopped jalapeño pepper
- 2 tablespoons minced fresh marjoram
- 2 tablespoons minced fresh parsley
- 1 egg, well beaten
- 2 tablespoons canola oil
- 1 tablespoon butter

1. Combine all the ingredients except the oil and butter in a medium-size bowl. Mold the mixture into small patties.
2. Heat the oil and butter in a nonstick skillet over medium heat. Sauté the patties until the chicken is thoroughly cooked and patties are golden brown, about 4 minutes on each side.

For the Corn Pancakes

- 1 cup white cornmeal
- ½ teaspoon salt
- 1 tablespoon maple syrup
- 1 cup boiling water
- 1 egg
- 1 cup low-fat milk or buttermilk
- 1 tablespoon canola oil
- 1 teaspoon baking powder
- 1 teaspoon baking soda
- 1 tablespoon minced savory
- 1 cup corn cut from the cob (raw or leftover cooked)
- Scant tablespoon canola oil for pan

1. Place the cornmeal, salt, and syrup in a medium-size bowl. Stir in the boiling water. Cover and let sit 10 minutes.
2. Combine the egg, milk, and oil in a bowl, and whisk until well blended.
3. Add the baking powder, baking soda, and savory, then stir in the corn kernels.
4. Blend the egg mixture into the cornmeal mixture. Add a little more milk if the batter seems too thick.
5. Heat a nonstick skillet over medium heat. Add just enough oil to coat the bottom of the pan. Fry the batter until top bubbles, flip and fry until underside is browned.
6. Serve hot with maple syrup and Chicken Sausage.

Wrap It Up

The term "wrap" encompasses a wide variety of edible "wrappers" used to package foods into pick-up fare. If you order a wrap in a restaurant, you'll probably get a tortilla or flatbread spread with a filling and then rolled up and cut into several sausage-size pieces. Variations abound, including Middle Eastern pita and lavash, Indian chapati and naan, and Asian rice paper and nori seaweed. Instead of a bread, you can also choose leafy vegetables to wrap around your filling. For instance, try large lettuce leaves or slightly steamed cabbage leaves. Several recipes featured in this book would make excellent stuffings for wraps. You may wish to try Rosemary Lima Bean Spread (page 24), Rosemary-Roasted Peppers (page 70), Chicken Sausage (page 52) with Mango Salsa (page 45), and Mexican Chicken Salad (page 54).

Mexican Chicken Salad

SERVES 6

Great for a summer picnic, this chicken salad is wonderful paired with a plate of sliced tomatoes sprinkled with basil, olive oil and vinegar, and salt and pepper to taste. Barely cooked corn cut fresh from the cob makes a wonderful accompaniment to this recipe. For another fresh touch, grind your own cumin: Simply toast cumin seeds in a heavy skillet over medium-low heat until they are fragrant, then grind them using a mortar and pestle. If you'd like to try a vegetarian variation of this same recipe, it's very tasty made with marinated or baked tofu instead of the chicken breast. Add chopped tomatoes and sweet peppers if you like.

1½ pounds boneless, skinless chicken breast
1 can (15 ounces) black beans, drained
1½ cups corn
2 tablespoons olive oil
3 cloves garlic, finely minced
½ cup diced scallions
½ cup finely minced parsley or cilantro
1 tablespoon finely minced fresh marjoram
1½ teaspoons ground cumin
2 tablespoons rice or white wine vinegar
½ teaspoon salt or 1 teaspoon Cajun Blend (page 13)

1. Place the chicken breasts in a medium-size skillet or saucepan. Add enough boiling water to cover. Bring water to a simmer, then cook over low heat, turning once. Cook until just done, about 4 minutes on each side. Drain and cool.

2. Cut cooked chicken into cubes, and place them in a large bowl. Add the remaining ingredients and mix well. Chill until serving time.

Marjoram

Baked Fish Steaks with Lemon Thyme

SERVES 4

Even folks who claim they don't like fish enjoy this dish, especially with basmati rice and Watermelon and Honeydew Salsa with Spearmint (page 45). Mako shark is a good choice if you like fish, or substitute pressed tofu if you wish.

> 2 pounds fresh fish steaks
> 1 tablespoon plain nonfat yogurt
> 1 tablespoon lemon zest
> 1 tablespoon finely minced lemon thyme
> ½ cup unsweetened apple or white grape juice

1. Preheat the oven to 450°F. Line a baking sheet with heavy-duty aluminum foil, using a piece large enough to wrap and seal the fish.
2. Place the fish on the foil, and brush it with the yogurt. Mix the lemon zest and herbs in a small bowl. Sprinkle the herb mixture over the fish. Bring the foil up around the fish. Pour the fruit juice around the fish, then seal the foil over the fish.
3. Bake for 20 minutes. Test for doneness: The fish should be cooked through, but still slightly pink inside. Serve piping hot.

Center-Stage Herbs

Don't forget to feature the complementary colors and fragrances of fresh herbs when you make flower arrangements. Try floating flower blossoms, such as pansies, chamomile, and roses, in shallow crystal bowls of water. It's fun to see the flower faces "up close and personal," and the effect is very cooling, as well.

For gathered arrangements, try orange mint with daisies; nasturtium leaves and flowers; spires of bergamot, lavender, or salvia; or sprays of sunny gold calendulas — perfect with opal basil!

Lemony Shrimp with Pasta

SERVES 4

Here's a festive dish that looks as though you spent hours in the kitchen. The only time-consuming step is peeling the shrimp. Buy a half-dozen extra with which to bribe the sous-chef!

For the Marinade
>   Juice of 1 lemon
>   1 tablespoon olive oil
>   2 tablespoons finely minced rosemary
>   2 garlic cloves, minced
>   ½ teaspoon salt
>   ⅛ teaspoon cayenne powder
>   1 pound peeled fresh shrimp

For the Pasta
>   1 pound linguine
>   6 stalks lemongrass
>   ¼ cup extra-virgin olive oil
>   Zest and juice of 1 lemon
>   ½–¾ cup Parmesan cheese
>   ¼ cup finely minced fresh parsley
>   Freshly ground black pepper, to taste

1. Combine all the marinade ingredients (except the shrimp) in a medium-size bowl. Add the shrimp and mix well to coat.
2. Refrigerate shrimp for at least 30 minutes, or up to 8 hours.
3. Heat a nonstick skillet over medium-high heat. Toss the shrimp in the marinade to coat thoroughly, strain out most of the marinade, and sauté for 4 to 5 minutes.
4. Cook the pasta with the lemongrass until the pasta is done. Discard the lemongrass, but reserve ½ cup of the cooking liquid.
5. Toss the pasta with the remaining ingredients and cooked shrimp, adding a little of the reserved cooking water from the pasta if needed. Serve immediately.

Fettucine with Garlicky Zucchini

SERVES 4

Many summer vegetables work well in this quick from-the-garden pasta dish. Instead of the zucchini, try julienned carrots, kohlrabi, green beans, or eggplant. Arugula and radicchio are also wonderful in it; shred the raw vegetables or use leftovers, stir-frying them briefly with the garlic to reheat. Substitute pumpkin seeds or pine nuts for the walnuts if you'd like.

> 1 pound zucchini, cut into 2-inch julienne strips
> ¼ cup olive oil
> 6–8 garlic cloves, finely minced
> ¾ pound fettucine
> 3 tablespoons finely minced fresh parsley
> 3 tablespoons finely minced garlic chives
> 2 tablespoons finely minced marjoram
> 1 tablespoon lemon juice or herb vinegar
> ½ cup grated Parmesan cheese, plus additional for topping
> ⅓ cup chopped English walnuts, toasted
> Freshly ground black pepper, to taste

1. Steam the zucchini until just tender, 3 to 5 minutes. Reserve.
2. Heat the olive oil in a small, nonstick skillet over medium-low heat. Add the garlic and sauté until golden brown, being careful not to burn. Remove from heat.
3. Cook the pasta until al dente, then drain, reserving ½ cup of the cooking liquid.
4. Toss the pasta with the zucchini, garlic, herbs, lemon juice or vinegar, and grated cheese. Add a little of the reserved cooking water if needed to coat the pasta. Top with the toasted walnuts. Season with pepper, and serve with more grated cheese.

Garlic chives

Basil-Parsley Pesto with Pumpkin Seeds

SERVES 6

It's worth it to take the time to strip the herb leaves from the stems for this fragrant summer main dish pesto and pasta. You can make the pesto several days ahead and refrigerate it until you're ready to serve. I prefer the more flavorful flat-leaved Italian parsley for this dish. If you don't have sorrel, add a teaspoon more of lemon juice. Although pine nuts are traditional, I like toasted pumpkin seeds. They're more nutritious and also less expensive.

For the Pesto

3 cups packed fresh Italian parsley leaves

1 cup packed fresh basil leaves

3–4 small sorrel leaves, if available

1 teaspoon salt

3–4 cloves garlic, peeled and coarsely chopped

¾ cup olive oil

1 tablespoon lemon juice

¼ cup freshly grated Parmesan cheese, plus additional for topping

For the Pasta

1½ pounds linguine

Freshly ground black pepper, to taste

¼ cup dry toasted pumpkin seeds

1. Place half of the pesto herbs in a food processor. Sprinkle with the salt and garlic. Process until everything is coarsely chopped. Add the remaining pesto herbs and process until uniformly chopped.

2. With the motor running, pour the olive oil into the processor in a thin stream. Process until well combined, 1 or 2 minutes. Add the lemon juice and cheese. Process 1 minute more. Hold the pesto in the food processor container until the pasta is ready.

3. Cook the pasta according to package directions.

4. While pasta is cooking, toast pumpkin seeds in a small, heavy skillet. Remove them from the heat when they begin to pop.

5. Drain the pasta, reserving ½ cup of the liquid. Turn the pasta into a large serving bowl.

6. Process the pesto for a few seconds more with ¼ cup of the reserved pasta water. Pour the sauce over the linguine. Toss, adding more pasta water if needed to distribute pesto evenly. Season with pepper, and sprinkle with the pumpkin seeds and extra cheese. Serve immediately.

Black-Skillet Corn Bread

MAKES 4 GENEROUS PIECES

An 8-inch cast-iron skillet is the secret weapon in this comforting dish of my grandfather's. If you don't have buttermilk, add 1 tablespoon of lemon juice or herb vinegar to nonfat milk to equal 1 cup. Sometimes I skip the maple syrup and bake ¼ cup Hot Pepper Jelly (page 21) into the corn bread. When I do, I also substitute 1 teaspoon of fresh savory or rosemary for the marjoram.

1 cup buttermilk	1 scant teaspoon salt
1 egg	1 tablespoon coarsely chopped
1 tablespoon maple syrup	fresh marjoram
1 cup white cornmeal	1 tablespoon butter
1 teaspoon baking soda	

1. Preheat oven to 450°F.

2. Whisk together the buttermilk, egg, and syrup in a medium-size bowl until the egg is well beaten.

3. Measure the dry ingredients and the marjoram in another bowl, and stir to combine. Pour the cornmeal mix into the liquid mix, and whip lightly to combine.

4. When the oven is hot, put the butter in a skillet and place it in the oven. Set the timer for 2 or 3 minutes so you don't forget to remove the pan before the butter burns. Remove the skillet from the oven — the butter should be bubbling. (Use a heavy pot holder!) Immediately pour the batter into the skillet. Bake 15 to 20 minutes, or until corn bread is golden brown.

One-Bowl Blueberry Cake

ONE 8-INCH SQUARE OR ROUND LAYER

Although this last-minute dessert doesn't need icing, it's delicious with Simple Orange Icing. Use chopped peaches instead of blueberries when they're in season.

¾ cup milk

5–6 lemon verbena leaves (fresh or dried) *or* 6 sprigs fresh lemon balm leaves

5 tablespoons softened, unsalted butter

¾ cup brown sugar

1 egg

1 teaspoon vanilla

1¾ cups unbleached flour

2 teaspoons baking soda

¼ teaspoon salt

¼ teaspoon ground nutmeg

1 cup fresh blueberries

1. Heat milk until it is hot but not boiling. Stir in whole lemon verbena leaves. Cover and let steep until milk reaches room temperature. Strain out herb leaves and discard. Reserve the milk.

2. Preheat the oven to 350°F. Grease and flour a cake pan.

3. In a medium-size bowl, cream butter and sugar. Beat in egg and vanilla.

4. Combine the dry ingredients in another bowl, and stir to mix. Add the flour mixture and milk alternately to the egg mixture, beginning and ending with the milk. Beat for a minute or two, or until smooth.

5. Fold in the blueberries. Turn the batter into the prepared pan.

6. Bake for 25 to 30 minutes, or until the cake tests done. Allow the cake to cool slightly in the pan for several minutes and then turn it onto a wire rack to cool. Frost if desired.

For Simple Orange Icing

1 tablespoon softened unsalted butter

1 tablespoon orange juice concentrate

1 cup confectioners' sugar

With an electric mixer, beat all ingredients until smooth. Icing should be thin. Spread on the cooled cake, allowing the icing to drizzle down the sides.

CHAPTER 4

AUTUMN
Recipes

arvesttime: Market stands overflow with a
carnival of pumpkins, winter squash, apples,
garlic, sweet potatoes, and Indian corn. It's
the last call for summer squash, tomatoes, and
peppers — suddenly precious, now that chilling winds have
crept through the fields. The scent of warm herbs wafts
through the kitchen — rosemary, sage, thyme, and bay.
Hardy cool-weather greens like parsley, cilantro, and chervil,
and wildings like dandelions, cress, and chicory are making a
fresh comeback. Now is the time to gather in the great
energy of spring and summer represented in the garden vegetables, grains, and herbs that soaked up the sun's vitality.
Properly stored and prepared, these potent gifts will warm us
through the winter.

61

Roasted Garlic and Herb Olives

SERVES 8 FOR APPETIZERS

My first taste of this festive dish was at our annual family reunion on Lake Erie. Serve with baguettes as a special-occasion appetizer. To avoid burns, let sit until cool enough to handle comfortably.

    4 heads garlic, unpeeled
    1 pound Greek calamata olives
    ½ pound oil-cured black olives
    3 Thai hot peppers, fresh or dried
    2 strips (2 inches each) fresh orange peel
    2 strips (2 inches each) fresh lemon peel
    2 sprigs each (2 inches apiece) fresh sage, rosemary, and thyme
    1 tablespoon fennel seeds
  2½–3 cups olive oil, to cover

1. Preheat the oven to 450°F.
2. Place the garlic, olives, and seasonings in a 2-quart heatproof casserole. Cover with the olive oil.
3. Bake 20 to 25 minutes, or until the oil is bubbly and fragrant, and the garlic is soft. Serve warm or at room temperature.

Luscious Leftovers

Roasted garlic: Squeeze flesh into a small crock, and cover with a film of oil. Refrigerate for up to 10 days. Garlic paste is great for stir-frying, rubbing on chicken before baking, or enriching dressings and marinades.

Olives: Store olives in a closed glass jar, refrigerated, for up to 2 weeks. Enjoy as is or snip them fine and toss with pasta and chopped parsley, hard-cooked egg, grated lemon rind, and enough oil to coat the pasta.

Marinade oil: Strain oil and store refrigerated in a glass bottle for up to 3 weeks. Use for stir-fry, salad dressing, marinade, and other sauces. Try marinating fresh goat cheese overnight with fresh rosemary and thyme sprigs.

Rosemary-Roasted Jerusalem Artichokes

SERVES 4

Jerusalem artichokes (also called sunchokes) thrive in some of the worst conditions, even in petrified clay soil. This recipe makes a finger-licking-good appetizer out of these indomitable plants. The only time-consuming job is scrubbing the tubers clean. If you don't have 'chokes, you can prepare sliced potatoes in the same manner with tasty results.

>   2 pounds unpeeled Jerusalem artichokes, cut
>   into 2-inch pieces
>   1–2 tablespoons olive oil
>   ¼ cup coarsely chopped fresh or dried rosemary
>   1 teaspoon salt

Rosemary

1. Preheat the oven to 425°F.
2. Mix the artichoke pieces with the olive oil. Spread the artichokes in a single layer on a baking sheet. Sprinkle with the rosemary and salt.
3. Bake 25 to 30 minutes, or until tender. Serve hot — with plenty of napkins.

Roasted Vegetable Treats

Roasted vegetables are hot! Cooking vegetables at a high temperature intensifies flavors, transforming ho-hum into yum. Resinous shrubby herbs like rosemary, sage, thyme, and bay are natural companions for vegetables. Use the recipe for Jerusalem artichokes to experiment with carrots, beets, parsnips, turnips, potatoes, Brussels sprouts, onions, and winter squash. No need to peel the vegetables — the skins hold in flavor.
  Vary the herbs to your liking.

Savory Spaghetti Squash Salsa

MAKES 5 CUPS

Salsa lovers of all ages will enjoy this autumn twist! Kids like to scoop out the spaghetti-like strands of this easy-to-grow winter squash, which stores well all winter.

1 medium-size spaghetti squash
1 cup peeled and diced plum
  tomatoes (about 2–3)
1 can (15 ounces) black beans,
  rinsed and drained
2 cloves garlic, finely minced
1 jalapeño pepper, finely minced
¼ cup lime juice
1 tablespoon balsamic or
  herb vinegar

2 tablespoons minced fresh
  parsley
1 tablespoon minced fresh
  marjoram
1 teaspoon dried savory
Pinch of sugar
Pinch of cayenne pepper
Salt and freshly ground black
  pepper, to taste

1. Preheat the oven to 350°F.
2. Cut squash in half lengthwise. Remove seeds. Place cut-sides down in a 9 × 13-inch baking dish. Add ½ inch of water to dish.
3. Bake for 45 minutes, or until the skin is tender to the touch. Cool.
4. Remove the flesh with a fork, and place it in a large mixing bowl. Add the remaining ingredients and combine well. Chill until serving time. Great with spicy corn chips.

Spicy Squash Seeds

Toast the seeds of any winter squash for a healthy snack. To prepare, separate the seeds from the fiber and wash clean. Drain. Spread the seeds on a greased baking sheet. Drizzle with a little olive oil and turn to coat. Sprinkle with salt or Cajun Blend (page 13). Bake in a 400°F oven for 20 minutes, or until golden brown, shaking the pan occasionally. Squash seeds keep better raw than toasted, so wait to toast them until you plan to use them.

Composed Autumn Salad

SERVES 4

The secret to cooking collards and kale is to julienne the greens so they cook quickly, retaining color and flavor but not toughness. Use a full-flavored vinegar for this dish — Opal Basil-Garlic-Black Peppercorn Vinegar (page 118) is good, as are balsamic vinegar and seasoned rice vinegar. When layering the salad, I like to add a final flourish of grated radish, ginger, or apple. Serve at room temperature or slightly chilled.

1 pound collard or kale greens
Splash of apple cider vinegar
⅓ cup olive oil
1 teaspoon toasted sesame oil
1 tablespoon tamari
2 tablespoons vinegar
1 cup uncooked sauerkraut
⅓ cup minced garlic chives

Optional garnishes: grated ginger, grated apple, grated radish, pomegranate seeds, halved black or red grapes, dried cranberries (soak first in sauerkraut juice to soften), toasted walnuts, pumpkin seeds, or other nuts

1. Wash the greens and strip the leafy parts from the tough inner stems. Roll the leaves lengthwise into long cigars. Using a sharp knife, cut the leaves crosswise into thin strips.

2. Bring a large pot of water to a boil. Add the julienned greens, stirring to submerge all of the leaves. Add a splash of vinegar. Return the water to boiling, uncovered, and set the timer for 5 minutes.

3. When the buzzer rings, taste-test the greens to make sure they're tender. Cook for a minute or two longer if necessary, but don't let them get mushy.

4. Pour the greens into a colander. Run cold water over them until they are cool to the touch. Let drain.

5. Put the oils, tamari, and 2 tablespoons of vinegar in a glass jar with a tight-fitting, nonmetal lid. When ready to serve, shake the dressing until it is well blended.

6. Compose the salad: first a layer of cooked greens, then a layer of sauerkraut; sprinkle the garlic chives and pour dressing to taste. Add optional garnish if desired.

Curried Sweet Potato Soup

SERVES 6–8

Here's a golden autumn recipe: calcium-rich sweet potatoes warmed with nourishing ginger, sage, and curry. Once you roast the sweet potatoes, the soup is ready to eat in 20 minutes. This is my family's favorite first course for Thanksgiving dinner. With crusty bread and a salad, this soup makes a hearty meal.

3 medium-to-large sweet potatoes
1 tablespoon olive oil, plus a little to rub on potatoes
1 Spanish onion, finely minced
1 teaspoon to 2 tablespoons prepared Indian curry paste, to taste
3 sage leaves, fresh or dried
2 tablespoons unsweetened coconut
1 tablespoon grated fresh ginger
1 tablespoon curry powder
4 cups water
2½ cups apple cider
Dollop of vanilla yogurt, for garnish

1. Preheat the oven to 425°F.
2. Scrub the sweet potatoes and rub them lightly with some olive oil. Place the potatoes on a rack in a roasting pan and bake for 45 minutes, or until soft. Cool and peel the potatoes.
3. Place a stockpot over medium heat. Add the rest of the olive oil. Sauté the minced onion in the hot oil until softened. Stir in the curry paste, sage leaves, coconut, ginger, and curry powder. Sauté for a few minutes to blend the flavors.
4. Add the meat from the peeled sweet potatoes. Sauté briefly. Stir in the water and apple cider. Reduce heat to low and simmer for 15 to 20 minutes.
5. Puree the soup in a blender before serving. A dollop of vanilla yogurt makes a cooling garnish. For a pretty spiderweb effect, thin the yogurt with a little apple cider, drizzle it in a spiral into each bowl, then use a table knife to cut through the spirals.

Mushroom Barley Soup

SERVES 6

A soul-satisfying soup for a dreary day. Eventually I'll learn how to harvest wild mushrooms in addition to the distinctive morels that grow in our woods near the wild ginseng. Meanwhile, I buy a mixed package of mushrooms for this soup. Shiitakes are also good. If using dried mushrooms, soak them first according to package directions.

2 tablespoons canola oil

2 large leeks (include tender part of green stalk), thinly sliced

1 cup finely chopped Spanish onion

1 cup finely chopped celery (include a few leaves)

2 cloves garlic, finely minced

½ cup barley

4½ cups water

¾ pound mushrooms

1 bay leaf

⅓ cup fresh parsley

2 tablespoons fresh thyme

Salt, to taste

Freshly grated nutmeg, for garnish

1. Heat the oil over medium-low heat in a large stockpot. Sauté the leeks, onion, celery, and garlic until they begin to soften.
2. Add the barley and sauté a few minutes more.
3. Add the water, mushrooms, and bay leaf. Bring to a boil. Reduce the heat and simmer covered for 45 minutes, or until the barley is tender. Turn off the heat.
4. Add the remaining seasonings, cover, and let sit for 15 minutes.
5. Puree half of the soup in a blender. Return the puree to the stockpot and blend with the remaining soup.
6. Serve steaming hot with fresh nutmeg grated over each bowl.

Thyme

Spicy Black Bean Turkey Chili with Winter Squash

SERVES 8

On a frosty fall night, this chili is rapturous paired with corn bread and Hot Pepper Jelly (page 21). Dried chipotles are worth keeping on hand for any southwestern-style bean dish. Many grocery stores keep them in stock, but if you can't find them, feel free to use another type of hot pepper, fresh or dried. One small butternut squash yields about 6 cups of diced flesh. If you have any frozen sweet corn, try adding a cup in the last few minutes of cooking. I like to ladle the soup over torn arugula greens to make a one-bowl meal.

1 teaspoon cumin seeds

2–3 jalapeño peppers, peeled and chopped

1 red bell pepper, peeled and chopped

2 tablespoons canola oil

6–8 cloves garlic, finely minced

1 large Spanish onion, chopped

1 pound ground turkey

1½ cups vegetable stock

6 cups peeled and cubed butternut squash

1 dried chipotle chili (optional)

1 tablespoon minced fresh sage

1 can black beans, rinsed and drained

4 tablespoons red wine vinegar, such as Opal Basil-Garlic-Black Peppercorn Vinegar (page 118) (optional)

1. Toast the cumin seeds over low heat in a small cast-iron skillet. Grind them with a mortar and pestle and reserve.
2. Roast and peel the peppers (see page 70). Reserve.
3. Heat the oil in a large saucepan over medium-low heat. Add the garlic, sauté for 1 minute, then add the onion and continue to sauté until the onion begins to soften.
4. Stir in the turkey and sauté until lightly browned.

5. Add stock, cubed squash, roasted peppers, and the optional chipotle chili. Cover and cook for 30 minutes.
6. Add the sage and drained beans. Cook 15 minutes more, or until the squash is tender. Add a splash of vinegar (about ½ tablespoon) to each bowl before serving if desired.

Broccoli with Lemon Thyme and Grapes

SERVES 4

'm always looking for a different way to serve this nutritious vegetable. You can also make this dish with Brussels sprouts. Either way, it pairs well with baked fish or chicken.

½ cup halved seedless grapes
2 teaspoons balsamic vinegar
1½–2 pounds fresh broccoli, cut into florets
1 tablespoon olive oil
2 cloves garlic, finely minced
1 medium onion, cut in ¼-inch-thick half-moons
½ cup vegetable stock or water
1 tablespoon minced fresh lemon thyme
¼ cup walnuts, coarsely chopped and toasted (optional)

1. Place the grapes in a small bowl. Stir in the vinegar and let sit while the broccoli cooks.
2. Steam the broccoli in a vegetable steamer over high heat for 2 to 3 minutes. Remove from the heat.
3. Heat the olive oil in a large skillet over medium-low heat. Add the garlic and sauté for 1 minute. Add the onion and sauté until it softens.
4. Stir in the stock or water. Add the broccoli and lemon thyme. Cover and simmer for 4 to 5 minutes, or until the broccoli is almost tender.
5. Stir in the grapes and simmer 1 minute more.
6. Serve garnished with toasted walnuts if desired.

Roasted Pepper Pitas

SERVES 4

Enjoy roasted red peppers in a pita sandwich, or marinate them in Autumn Walnut Vinaigrette and use as a topping for pizza, pasta, salads, or sandwiches.

2 tablespoons coarsely chopped walnuts

4 regular or onion pitas

1 cup chopped Rosemary-Roasted Peppers (see box)

½ cup crumbled feta cheese

1 teaspoon dried marjoram

A few arugula or watercress leaves

½ cup thinly sliced cucumbers

Autumn Walnut Vinaigrette (page 71)

Salt and freshly ground black pepper, to taste

1. Heat a cast-iron skillet and dry-toast the walnuts. Set aside.
2. Split the pitas with a fork or knife. Using a hot griddle or cast-iron skillet, grill the pitas for 1 or 2 minutes on each side.
3. Mix the walnuts, peppers, feta, and marjoram in a small bowl.
4. Line pitas with greens and cucumber slices. Stuff with pepper mixture. Drizzle with a generous amount of Autumn Walnut Vinaigrette. Season with salt and pepper to taste.

Rosemary-Roasted Peppers

Line a baking sheet with aluminum foil and spray with nonstick cooking spray. Cover the sheet with sprigs of rosemary. Select a colorful mixture of peppers, including hot peppers if desired. Cut bell types lengthwise into quarters, and arrange over rosemary. Place baking sheet directly under broiler. Check at 3 minutes, turn peppers, and broil 3 minutes more, or until they are evenly charred. Place peppers and rosemary in a paper bag and close. Let sit for 10 minutes; the steam makes skins easier to peel. Once peppers are cool, skin and seed them. Use immediately, or refrigerate for up to a week. Or, cut peppers into pieces, crumble some of the rosemary, and marinate all in Autumn Walnut Vinaigrette. Refrigerate for up to 10 days.

Autumn Walnut Vinaigrette

MAKES ABOUT ½ CUP

Mild and nutty flavored, this salad dressing is delicious with delicate mixed greens, such as mesclun. Autumn Walnut Vinaigrette also makes an excellent marinade for Rosemary-Roasted Peppers (page 70).

½ cup walnut oil
2 teaspoons lemon juice
1–2 tablespoons herb vinegar (See page 118; rosemary, shallots, and tarragon make a good combination.)
Salt and freshly ground black pepper

Combine all ingredients, and whisk or stir to mix well. Refrigerate.

End-of-the-Garden Pasta Toss

SERVES 4

If you had time to salvage some tomatoes and basil before Jack Frost ripped through the garden, here's a fragrant toast to the end of summer, perfect for a quick supper or weekend lunch.

1 tablespoon olive oil
2–4 cloves garlic, minced
2 cups coarsely chopped arugula
2–3 tomatoes, peeled and diced
1 pound linguine

4 ounces goat cheese, crumbled
2 tablespoons fresh marjoram
Salt and freshly ground black pepper, to taste
2 tablespoons coarsely chopped walnuts, dry-toasted

1. Heat the oil in a skillet over medium-low heat. Add the garlic and sauté for 1 or 2 minutes. Turn off heat. Stir in the arugula and the tomatoes. Cover to keep warm until the pasta is done.

2. Cook pasta according to package directions. Drain, reserving ¼ cup of cooking water, then place in a large serving bowl. Toss with vegetables, goat cheese, and marjoram. Add a little cooking water to blend ingredients well. Season with salt and pepper. Garnish with toasted walnuts. Serve hot.

Spinach Pesto Pizza

MAKES 4 MEDIUM-SIZE PIECES

reen or not, this is a satisfying combination that pleases all ages
and is a welcome change from the customary red pizza sauce. I
usually use purchased whole wheat flatbreads to reduce calories, but
if you have a favorite recipe for a big deep-dish pizza crust, this
makes a wonderful filling for it. Double the filling ingredients for a
family-size feast.

1 tablespoon basil puree or pesto (see pages 116 and 42)
1 flatbread (8 x 11 inches) or 1 pizza shell (12 inches)
¼ pound provolone cheese, thinly sliced
⅓ cup thinly sliced red onion
1 bunch (about 4 cups) fresh spinach
1 teaspoon lemon zest
2 cloves garlic, finely minced
1 teaspoon crumbled dried rosemary
Freshly ground black pepper, to taste
½ cup crumbled feta cheese
½ cup freshly grated Romano, pecorino, or Parmesan cheese

1. Preheat the oven to 400°F.
2. Spread the basil puree or pesto over the flatbread or pizza shell.
   Top with the provolone and then the onion slices. Set aside.
3. Heat a large skillet. Add the spinach and sauté only
   until spinach begins to wilt. Toss the spinach with
   the lemon zest, garlic, and rosemary. Drain
   excess liquid from the spinach.
4. Spread the spinach on the prepared crust.
   Sprinkle with a few generous grinds of
   pepper. Top with the remaining cheeses.
5. Bake for 15 to 20 minutes, or until
   cheeses are bubbly and golden brown.

Basil

Corn and Zucchini Fritters

S E R V E S 4

These delicate patties are easy to prepare, and they make a wonderful supper or Sunday brunch. The supper version is great with Chicken Sausage (page 52), cooked apples, and hot maple syrup. For an elegant brunch, serve with lox and sour cream (or yogurt) mixed with a little horseradish and garnished with minced chives.

2 small zucchini

1 teaspoon salt

1 cup buttermilk

1 large egg

½ cup corn kernels, fresh or frozen

½ teaspoon salt

1 teaspoon dried savory

⅛ teaspoon cayenne pepper

2 teaspoons baking soda

½ teaspoon baking powder

1 cup yellow cornmeal

Canola or peanut oil, for frying

1. Grate the zucchini and place in a large sieve set over a bowl. Sprinkle with 1 teaspoon salt. Let stand for 10 minutes, then squeeze out as much excess liquid as possible.
2. Beat the buttermilk with the egg in a medium bowl. Stir in the corn and zucchini.
3. Combine the dry ingredients in a larger bowl and mix well. Pour the zucchini mixture into the dry ingredients. Mix until just combined.
4. Heat the oil in a skillet. Fry fritters 2 to 3 minutes on one side, then flip and fry a minute or two longer, or until crispy and golden. Serve immediately.

Fennel and Rosemary-Roasted Chicken

S E R V E S 4

Prepare the marinade Saturday morning and you'll be ready for easy entertaining that night. I usually bake the chicken in a Dutch oven with quartered carrots and potatoes, but this recipe also works well on the grill.

For the Marinade
3 tablespoons lemon juice

¼ cup tamari or soy sauce

3 tablespoons olive oil

6 cloves garlic, finely minced

4 chicken breasts, boneless
and skinless

For the Herb Rub
1 teaspoon kosher salt

1 teaspoon black peppercorns

1 teaspoon crumbled, dried
lemon verbena

Pinch of cayenne pepper

1 tablespoon dried rosemary

1 tablespoon fennel seeds

Several rosemary sprigs

1. Combine the lemon juice, tamari or soy sauce, oil, and garlic in a small bowl. Whisk well to blend.

2. Place the chicken in a large bowl. Pour the marinade over the chicken, and turn the pieces to coat. Cover and refrigerate for at least 2 hours. Turn several times to marinate evenly.

3. Preheat the oven to 425°F.

4. Grind the salt, peppercorns, lemon verbena, cayenne, rosemary, and fennel seeds in a food processor or with a mortar and pestle.

5. Remove the chicken from the marinade, shaking off any excess liquid. (Discard the marinade.) Place the chicken pieces in a roasting pan and sprinkle with the seasoning mix. Tuck the rosemary sprigs under the chicken pieces.

6. Cover the roasting pan and bake 20 to 25 minutes, or until chicken juices run clear.

Fennel

Baked Fish with Zested Parsley

S E R V E S 4

This simple recipe never fails. Coating the fish with yogurt keeps it moist without adding unnecessary fat. A little liquid added to the baking pan steams the fish, which also helps to keep it moist.

> 2 pounds flounder, halibut, cod, or other white fish
>
> 2 tablespoons plain, nonfat yogurt
>
> Zest from 1 lemon
>
> ½ cup chopped fresh flat-leaf parsley leaves
>
> 1 tablespoon minced fresh chervil
>
> 1 tablespoon minced fresh lemon thyme
>
> 2 cloves garlic, finely minced
>
> ½ teaspoon salt
>
> Pinch of cayenne pepper
>
> ½ cup unsweetened apple or white grape juice

1. Preheat the oven to 400°F.
2. Spray a 9 × 13-inch ovenproof baking dish with cooking spray. Place the fish in the baking dish and coat with the yogurt.
3. Blend the lemon zest, parsley, chervil, lemon thyme, garlic, salt, and cayenne in a small bowl. Sprinkle over the fish. Pour the fruit juice around the fish. Cover the dish with foil.
4. Bake for 20 minutes, or until fish flakes.

Herbed Yogurt Cheese

Here's another use for yogurt. Line a sieve with a double layer of coffee filters, and place it over a bowl. Put 2 cups of nonfat plain yogurt in the sieve. Cover with plastic wrap, and let drain at room temperature for 24 to 36 hours. Mix the resulting cheese with 1 teaspoon dry vegetable broth mix, 1 to 2 finely minced shallots, 1 tablespoon minced fresh parsley, 2 teaspoons minced fresh marjoram, and salt and pepper. A great spread for bagels!

Marinated Turkey Breast

SERVES 4–6

For a small Thanksgiving dinner, roast a turkey breast. It tastes delicious and makes great leftovers for sandwiches. When ready to cook, fire up the grill if the weather permits, or place the meat in a roasting bag and bake. Rosemary honey (see page 22) is terrific in this recipe.

3- to 5-pound turkey breast
1 cup tamari or soy sauce
½ cup lemon juice
¼ cup honey
¼ cup peanut or sunflower oil
1 tablespoon toasted sesame oil
2 tablespoons Poultry Seasoning (page 11)
Handful of rosemary sprigs

1. Place the turkey breast in a large self-sealing or heavy-duty plastic bag, and set the bagged turkey in a pan or bowl to avoid leakage.
2. Mix the tamari or soy sauce, lemon juice, honey, and oils in a small bowl. Pour this mixture into the bag, over the turkey. Marinate 8 to 12 hours, turning the bag occasionally to distribute the marinade.
3. Remove the turkey from the marinade. Discard any leftover marinade.
4. Sprinkle the turkey generously with Poultry Seasoning. If grilling, stuff rosemary sprigs under the skin of the turkey, trying not to split the skin. If using a roasting bag, place the rosemary in the bag along with the turkey.
5. Preheat the oven to 350°F. For oven roasting, cook turkey about 20 minutes per pound, or until the internal temperature at the thickest part of the breast registers 180°F on a meat thermometer. Let stand in the roasting bag for 10 minutes before removing. For grilling, roast 10 to 15 minutes on each side, then place cover on grill and cook about 20 to 30 minutes longer.

Seeded Sweet Potato Biscuits

MAKES ABOUT 1 DOZEN LARGE BISCUITS

Homemade biscuits are a real treat with cold-weather soups and stews. Serve homemade herb butter (see page 13) with them. They're also good with scrambled eggs, especially when slathered with Rosemary-Goldenrod Jelly (page 22) or an herbal honey (see page 22).

½ cup raw, shelled sunflower seeds
2 cups unbleached flour
1 tablespoon brown sugar
2 teaspoons baking soda
1 teaspoon baking powder
2 teaspoons coarsely chopped fresh rosemary
1 tablespoon ground coriander seed
1 tablespoon orange zest
1 heaping teaspoon ground nutmeg
1 heaping teaspoon ground cinnamon
½ cup cold unsalted butter, cut into tiny pieces
1 cup mashed cooked sweet potato
½ cup milk

1. Preheat the oven to 375°F.
2. Place the dry ingredients in a food processor. Pulse until the sunflower seeds and rosemary are coarsely ground. Add the butter and pulse a few more times — enough to cut the butter into the flour mixture.
3. Add the sweet potato and half the milk and pulse again. Add enough of the remaining milk to make a batter that holds together.
4. Drop heaping tablespoonfuls of the dough on a greased baking sheet. With floured hands, pat biscuits into shape.
5. Bake 15 to 20 minutes, or until golden brown.

Coriander

Cinnamon Basil Applesauce Cake

MAKES ONE 10-INCH TUBE CAKE

One of my favorite cakes, this herbed applesauce cake can be glazed or not. Instead of cinnamon basil, try lemon verbena or lemon balm for a different, but equally delicious, taste.

For the Cake
- 4 cups peeled and sliced tart apples
- 6 sprigs (2 inches each) cinnamon basil
- 2 cups currants
- 3½ cups unbleached flour
- 1½ cups sugar
- 2 teaspoons ground cinnamon
- 1 teaspoon ground ginger
- 1 teaspoon ground cloves

½ cup chopped black walnuts
¾ cup vegetable shortening
4 teaspoons baking soda, dissolved in 1 cup lukewarm water

For the Cinnamon Basil Icing
- ½ cup packed cinnamon basil leaves
- ¼ cup boiling water
- 1 tablespoon softened unsalted butter
- 1½ cups confectioners' sugar
- 1 teaspoon lemon zest

1. Preheat the oven to 350°F. Grease a 10-inch tube pan.
2. Place the apples in a large saucepan. Cover and cook gently until apples are soft. Remove from heat, add the cinnamon basil sprigs, cover, and let sit for 20 minutes. Remove the cinnamon basil.
3. Whip the apples briskly with a whisk to make a coarse applesauce. Stir in the currants. Cover the pan again to keep warm.
4. Mix flour, sugar, spices, and nuts in a large bowl. Add shortening to the hot applesauce, and stir until it melts. Add the baking soda water to the applesauce. Pour the applesauce mixture into the flour mixture. Mix until well blended. Pour into the prepared pan.
5. Bake 1¼ hours, or until a toothpick inserted in the cake comes out clean. Remove it from the pan and cool.
6. For the icing, in a small saucepan, steep the cinnamon basil leaves in the boiling water for 20 minutes. Remove the leaves and simmer the infusion for a few minutes to reduce the liquid by half. Let cool.
7. Beat the butter, sugar, and lemon zest. Add enough cinnamon basil infusion to make a thin glaze. Pour it over the cooled cake.

CHAPTER 5

WINTER

Recipes

T he solstice marks the beginning of winter in my part of the world. After the celebratory flurry of holiday visiting and rich treats, it feels good to sit back and stir a simple pot of bean soup.

I enjoy the quietness of winter more each passing year. With not as much to do, I'm more content to be, well, a human being rather than a human doing. Cooking is a more relaxed affair, as the kitchen heat and penetrating fragrances of rosemary, bay, and thyme invite me to linger and then to call a friend to share scones and Rosemary-Goldenrod Jelly (page 22) with herbal tea. I like to putter in the kitchen making dried herb blends (see page 11) and herb butters (see page 13). This is a good time to inventory the pantry and freezer, and dig into the winter stash with less caution.

Texas Caviar

SERVES 8

Black-eyed peas are traditional southern fare for New Year's Day. For this updated version, use Opal Basil-Garlic-Black Peppercorn Vinegar (page 118). Serve with tortilla chips or grilled pitas.

1½ cups dried black-eyed peas
1 sprig (3 inches) sage
1 dried chipotle chili
3 cups boiling water
4 scallions, minced (use some of the green)
2–3 roasted jalapeño peppers, peeled, seeded, and chopped

⅓ cup walnut or peanut oil
¼ cup apple cider or herb vinegar
¼ cup lime juice
Salt and freshly ground black pepper, to taste
⅓ cup packed, minced fresh cilantro

1. Wash the peas, discarding any that are imperfect. Place the peas in a 3-quart saucepan with the sage and chili. Stir in the boiling water. Return to a boil, cover, and adjust heat to a gentle simmer. Cook for 35 to 45 minutes, or until peas are tender but not mushy.
2. Whisk the remaining ingredients in a small bowl. Pour over peas, and stir until well combined; then pour into a bowl and cover.
3. Marinate peas in the refrigerator at least overnight — three days is better. Serve chilled or at room temperature.

Rosemary Chickpea Appetizer Bake

SERVES 4–6

What a wonderful, finger-licking dish to share with good friends! Mix the batter early in the day so you can pop it in the oven when guests arrive. Hot Pepper Jelly (page 21) makes a delicious dipping sauce! Serve as soon as it's cool enough to handle, by breaking it apart and eating it with your fingers.

1½ cups water
1 cup chickpea flour
4 tablespoons olive oil

½ teaspoon salt
1 tablespoon chopped fresh rosemary
Lots of freshly ground black pepper

1. Pour the water into a medium-size bowl. Whisk in the chickpea flour until lumps disappear. Let sit for 3 to 4 hours.
2. Preheat oven to 500°F. Pour the oil into an 11 × 15-inch metal baking pan. Turn pan to coat bottom.
3. Whisk the salt and rosemary into the chickpea flour mixture. Spread the mixture evenly in the pan. It should be no more than ¼ inch thick. Bake 20 minutes.
4. Remove the pan from the oven and sprinkle with the freshly ground pepper while it's still hot. May be stored for several weeks in the refrigerator.

Roasted Squash Butter

MAKES ABOUT 3 CUPS

Delicious served as a dip with crisp celery sticks or garlic toast, squash butter also makes a satisfying low-calorie spread for muffins and other breads. Store, refrigerated, for at least a week. You can also make this recipe using sweet potatoes or carrots.

3–4 sprigs fresh sage	½ teaspoon dried marjoram
1 medium butternut squash	2 tablespoons tahini
1 small onion, finely minced	3 tablespoons barley miso
2 cloves garlic, finely minced	(available at natural-food
1 tablespoon olive oil	stores)

1. Preheat oven to 425°F.
2. Line a roasting pan with aluminum foil and spray with nonstick cooking spray. Lay the sage sprigs in the pan.
3. Cut the squash in half lengthwise. Clean out the seeds. Place the squash cut-sides down over the sage leaves. Bake 45 minutes, or until the squash is soft to the touch. Cool.
4. Sauté the onion and garlic in the oil over medium heat until they turn light brown. Reserve.
5. Remove the flesh from the squash and place it in a food processor with the cooked onion and garlic and the remaining ingredients. Process until smooth. This dip is best served at room temperature.

Caramelized Onion Sauce

MAKES 3–4 CUPS

Fragrant onions and thyme, cooked until sweetly savory, are delicious as a spread on chewy herbed breads. For a special treat, grill Swiss cheese on pumpernickel bread, cut into wedges, and let guests slather the onion sauce on top. You can also toss it with pasta, spread it on pizza, or use it as a sauce for grilled fish or meats. It's even great on a simple cheese omelet. Use the heaviest skillet in the house to help prevent the onions from scorching.

3 tablespoons olive oil
5 large Spanish onions, thinly sliced
6–8 cloves garlic, finely minced

1 cup apple cider
1 teaspoon balsamic vinegar
¼ cup fresh, finely minced thyme
Salt and pepper, to taste

1. Heat the olive oil in a heavy skillet over medium heat. Add the onions and garlic. (If your skillet is small, you can add the onions in small amounts, continuing to add more as they cook down.) Lower heat to a gentle simmer and stir. Cook, uncovered, until the onions are golden in color and greatly reduced in volume — about 1 hour. Stir frequently to prevent scorching.
2. Add the cider, vinegar, and thyme, and cook until the liquid has been absorbed. Season to taste with the salt and pepper.

Herbal Christmas Tree

Wrap an upside-down, circular tomato cage with grapevines, string white lights, and festoon with fragrant branches of rosemary or sage. You can add natural ornaments such as mini-grapevine wreaths decorated with dried garlic chive flower heads and wild rose hips; potpourri-covered balls; and tiny tussie-mussies wrapped in lamb's ears leaves for doilies.

Orange Onion Salad

S E R V E S 4

When temple oranges are at their peak, this colorful combination of tart and sweet flavors is my favorite salad. It's so refreshing in the midst of heavier winter foods.

4 cups fresh spinach or arugula leaves
⅓ cup fruity olive oil
1 teaspoon toasted sesame oil
1 tablespoon balsamic vinegar
1 teaspoon dried marjoram
Pinch of sugar
2 tablespoons sesame seeds
4 sweet oranges, peeled, seeded, and cut into thin slices
1 cup very thinly sliced Vidalia or red onion (more or less to taste)
Freshly ground black pepper, to taste

1. Wash, dry, and chill the greens.
2. Mix the oils, vinegar, marjoram, and sugar in a small glass jar. Shake to combine.
3. Toast the sesame seeds in a small cast-iron skillet. Reserve.
4. To assemble the salad, place greens on four salad plates. Add a layer of oranges, then a layer of onions. Shake the dressing ingredients to blend again and pour over the salad. Sprinkle with toasted sesame seeds and a few grinds of pepper.

Wintry Herbs

Although I visit the freezer for herb paste and occasionally splurge on cilantro from the market, I find the "wintry" herbs more appealing for cold-weather cooking. For instance, I find that herbs like rosemary, sage, and thyme have a warming effect on the body, whereas basil, dill, and cilantro have a cooling effect.

Warm Salad of Leeks and Collards with Tahini

SERVES 4–6

Here's another savory twist on cooked greens, so heartening during the winter months. I like this any time of day: for breakfast with toast, with garlic toast for lunch, or as a side dish with dinner.

1 large bunch collards, julienned, 5–6 cups
1 tablespoon olive oil
6–8 cloves garlic, finely minced
2 large leeks, white part cut into thin rounds
3 tablespoons Opal Basil-Garlic-Black Peppercorn Vinegar (page 118)
⅓ cup tahini
1 tablespoon tamari or soy sauce
¼ cup minced garlic chives

1. Bring an 8-quart stockpot of water to a boil.
2. Clean the collards and remove the tough inner rib. Roll the leaves lengthwise and cut them crosswise into thin strips.
3. Cook the greens in boiling water for 3 to 4 minutes, until almost tender. Drain them in a colander, and run cold water over them to cool. Reserve.
4. Heat the oil in a large skillet over medium-low heat. Sauté the garlic and leeks until they begin to soften. Stir in the collards, add the vinegar, tahini, and tamari or soy sauce, and sauté until collards are heated through. Stir in the garlic chives. Serve warm.

Winter Substitute for Chives

In central Maryland, I can scavenge garlic mustard (*Alliaria officinalis*) from the woods' edge all winter. If this plant grows in your area, cut a handful of the round leaves, remove the stems, and chop the leaves finely. Use it as you would chives, raw or lightly cooked, to add a mild garlic flavor to soups, salads, herb butter, softened cheeses, and other savories.

Clam Stew

My mother has always been a pioneer. Although she grew up in the days when everything was deep-fried, Mom was inspired by healthy eating long before it became popular. This '60s recipe empties more cans than either of us would use now, but it's quick, nutritious, delicious, and rich in warm memories. Herb butter (see page 13) makes an elegant finish for the stew. It's also delicious as a spread on bread or crackers.

3 medium potatoes, scrubbed (not peeled) and cut into bite-size pieces

2 medium onions, chopped

3 stalks celery, including some of the leaves, chopped

2 carrots, scrubbed (not peeled) and cut into rounds

2 bay leaves

3 cans (8.5 ounces) minced clams, undrained

2 bottles (8 ounces) clam juice

1 can (15 ounces) low-fat creamed corn

1 box (10 ounces) frozen peas

2 teaspoons dried thyme

1 teaspoon dried marjoram

Salt and freshly ground black pepper, to taste

Thin slice of unsalted butter for each bowl

½ cup minced fresh parsley, chervil, and/or chives, for garnish

1. Place potatoes, onions, celery, carrots, and bay leaves in a large saucepan. Add enough water to barely cover. Bring to a boil, then adjust heat to a gentle simmer. Cover the pan and cook for 35 to 45 minutes, until vegetables are tender but not mushy.
2. Add the clams, clam juice, corn, peas, thyme, marjoram, salt, and pepper, and heat 15 minutes more.
3. Place a thin slice of butter in each bowl before ladling the soup into dishes. Garnish with the fresh minced herbs and a dot of herb butter, if desired.

Classy White-Bean Soup

SERVES 8

Dressed up with Garlic Butter Drizzle, and served with salad and good bread, this simple soup is ready for company. I generally use Great Northern beans or navy beans; cannellini beans are good, too. If you have a pressure cooker, the beans will be ready to puree in less than 1 hour. For a different twist, substitute last summer's frozen pesto, thawed and warmed, for the Garlic Butter Drizzle.

2 cups dried white beans

3 tablespoons olive oil

2 medium onions, chopped

2 shallots, finely minced

6 cups water or vegetable stock

2 bay leaves

3 sprigs (6 inches) fresh thyme

1 teaspoon dried savory

Salt and freshly ground black pepper, to taste

Fresh parsley, finely chopped, for garnish

For the Garlic Butter Drizzle

2 tablespoons olive oil

1 tablespoon unsalted butter

4 cloves garlic, finely minced

1. Soak the beans in water overnight. Drain and wash them until the water runs clear. Reserve.

2. Heat the oil in a large saucepan. Sauté the onions and shallots over medium-low heat until they begin to soften. Add the beans, water or stock, and bay leaves. Cook 2 to 3 hours, or until the beans are tender.

3. Stir in the thyme and savory. Cover the pan and let sit until it cools slightly (at least 15 minutes).

4. Remove the bay leaves and thyme sprigs. Puree the soup.

5. To make the Garlic Butter Drizzle, heat the oil and butter in a small skillet over medium heat. Sauté the garlic until it begins to turn golden brown. Remove from the heat.

6. Ladle the soup into bowls, add a little Garlic Butter Drizzle, and garnish with the parsley and salt and pepper to taste.

Roasted Herbed Cauliflower

SERVES 4–6

Serving the cauliflower whole creates an impressive dish that's deceptively simple to prepare. A large covered casserole dish or Dutch oven works best for roasting. Line the bottom with aluminum foil or parchment paper, as the honey may stick to the bottom of the pan. Alternatively, use a purchased roasting bag. Rosemary herb honey (see page 22) is excellent for this dish along with Opal Basil-Garlic-Black Peppercorn Vinegar (page 118).

1 perfect head of cauliflower
½ cup herb honey
1 teaspoon ground coriander seed
2 tablespoons grated fresh gingerroot
1 tablespoon herb vinegar
2 fresh bay leaves, torn into several pieces
1 teaspoon roasted sesame oil
½ teaspoon salt
1 teaspoon freshly ground black pepper
5–6 sprigs fresh rosemary or thyme
1 cup water

1. Preheat oven to 400°F.
2. Remove any greens from the cauliflower.
3. Mix the remaining ingredients, except the rosemary and water, in a small bowl to make the dressing.
4. Place the rosemary in the bottom of the lined roasting pan. Place the cauliflower in the pan, leafy-side down. Drizzle the head with the dressing. Pour the water into the bottom of the pan. Bake, covered, for 30 minutes.
5. Remove the pan from the oven to baste. Add more water if needed. Bake 20 minutes more, or until tender. Baste again.
6. Serve hot or at room temperature.

Bay

Broiled Onions and Portobello Mushrooms

SERVES 4

We enjoy this rich-tasting but low-calorie side dish with turkey burgers. It also makes a nice topping for pizza. Any leftovers are a fine addition to grilled cheese sandwiches or omelets.

> 1 large onion, thinly sliced
> 1–2 portobello mushrooms, thinly sliced
> 1–2 tablespoons olive oil
> 1–2 tablespoons tamari or soy sauce
> 1 tablespoon minced fresh thyme

1. Line a baking sheet with aluminum foil. Spread the onions and mushrooms over the foil. Drizzle with a little olive oil and tamari or soy sauce. Mix the vegetables around to coat evenly. Let sit for an hour. Sprinkle with the thyme.
2. Broil the marinated onions and mushrooms about 6 to 8 minutes. Turn the vegetables midway to ensure even browning. Serve hot.

Sagey Turkey Burgers

SERVES 4

These turkey burgers are the best! Ricotta cheese gives the turkey a smoother texture and miso deepens the flavor. Bake in a loaf if you prefer. We like turkey burgers with Broiled Onions and Portobello Mushrooms. If you're really hungry, open a jar of tomatoes and simmer them with a little dill or basil pesto as another side dish.

> 1 pound ground turkey
> 2 cups cooked rice
> ½ cup ricotta cheese
> 2 tablespoons dark barley miso
> ½ cup finely minced fresh sage
> Freshly ground black pepper, to taste

1. Combine all the ingredients in a mixing bowl. Shape into patties.
2. Spray the skillet with nonstick cooking spray. Fry the turkey burgers over medium heat, turning once, until done, about 8 to 10 minutes total. Serve hot on a toasted bun.

Sweet-and-Sour Glazed Chicken

SERVES 4

This is a nice change from plain roasted chicken. It's extra good served with basmati rice, sautéed spinach, and corn bread. Slide a few fat carrots or sweet potatoes into the roasting pan if you like. My family enjoys Hot Pepper Jelly, but orange marmalade spiked with 1 teaspoon dried tarragon or a sage-cider jelly is also good. Roasting the chicken in a Dutch oven is a quick way to achieve moist chicken, and the jelly doesn't burn.

Several large sprigs fresh rosemary or sage
1 chicken (3–5 pounds), cut into pieces
1 cup Hot Pepper Jelly (page 21)
4–6 cloves garlic, finely minced
1 tablespoon tamari or soy sauce
Paprika
Salt, to taste

Sage

1. Preheat oven to 400°F. Place the rosemary in the bottom of a Dutch oven. Lay the chicken pieces on the herbs.
2. Mix the jelly, garlic, and tamari or soy sauce in a small bowl. Pour the dressing over the chicken and turn to coat. Sprinkle the chicken with paprika and salt.
3. Cover and bake 25 to 30 minutes, or until juices run clear. The internal temperature of the chicken should be 190°F.

Broiled Ginger Miso Salmon

SERVES 4

Served with steaming basmati rice and braised chard, this salmon is a personal favorite. Select a thin fillet if possible — that way it won't be necessary to turn the salmon during cooking. To avoid having to turn a thicker cut, cover the fish loosely with aluminum foil until it is almost done, and then brown under the broiler.

1½–2 pounds salmon fillets

3 tablespoons dark barley miso

2 tablespoons grated fresh gingerroot

2–3 cloves garlic, finely minced

⅓ cup white wine

¼ cup water, if needed

Fresh minced dill, for garnish

1. Set the broiler rack 6 inches from the heat source. Line a broiling pan with aluminum foil and spray with nonstick cooking spray.
2. Place the salmon in the pan skin-side down.
3. Mix the remaining ingredients in a small bowl. Coat the salmon with the sauce. Broil 8 to 10 minutes, or until salmon is cooked through but not dry. Check midway and add ¼ cup of water to the pan if all the liquid is absorbed.
4. Serve hot on warmed plates garnished with the fresh dill.

Herbed Tamari Nuts

MAKES 1 POUND

Use any combination of nuts that you like to make this delicious snack. My favorite is almonds and sunflower seeds, which I mix with raisins when serving. If you include seeds like sunflower or pumpkin in the mix, coat them separately and add to the baking tray about 30 minutes into the cooking, as they take less time to roast.

1 large egg white

1 tablespoon herb honey

1 tablespoon tamari or soy sauce

¼ cup minced fresh rosemary or sage

1 pound nuts or seeds, raw and shelled

1. Preheat oven to 250°F.
2. Beat the egg white until frothy. Whisk in the honey, tamari or soy sauce, and herbs.
3. Pour the dressing over the nuts in a small bowl. Stir until the nuts are well coated. Spread in a single layer on a nonstick baking sheet or on a regular sheet lined with parchment paper.
4. Bake 1 hour, turning several times. Cool. Store in airtight tins.

Southwestern-Style Spoonbread

SERVES 6

Eggs and cheese and butter — mmm. This spoonbread isn't low in calories, but it's very good. If you don't have any marinated jalapeños, use canned green chilis. Use more or less cayenne, depending on how hot you like things. I serve this with Hot Pepper Jelly (page 21) and a tossed salad to rave reviews.

1 cup cornmeal	1 can (15 ounces) creamed corn
1 teaspoon baking soda	⅛ teaspoon cayenne pepper
1 teaspoon dried marjoram	*For the Filling*
2 eggs	1 cup shredded Monterey Jack
⅔ cup buttermilk	cheese
3 tablespoons unsalted butter, melted	⅓ cup marinated jalapeños (see page 70), or canned peppers

1. Preheat oven to 400°F. Butter a soufflé dish.
2. Mix the cornmeal, baking soda, and marjoram in a medium-size bowl.
3. Beat the eggs, buttermilk, and melted butter in another bowl. Add the creamed corn and cayenne pepper, and stir until well combined. Beat the cornmeal mixture into the egg mixture, stirring only until combined.
4. Pour half the batter into the baking dish. Sprinkle batter with the cheese and marinated jalapeños. Cover with the remaining batter.
5. Bake for 35 to 40 minutes, or until set.

Rose-Scented Geranium Valentine's Day Cake

MAKES TWO 8- OR 9-INCH LAYERS

Topped with Cream Cheese Icing decorated with candied herbs (see page 121) or candy Valentine hearts, and served with a dollop of vanilla ice cream covered with Melba Sauce, this is a special dessert for a very special somebody. Expect to be showered with sticky sweet kisses when you present it!

For even stronger rose flavor, use ¼ to ½ cup purchased rose water for part of the milk. Or, the day before you make the cake, wrap fresh rose-scented geranium leaves around the butter, and refrigerate overnight. Discard the leaves before softening the butter.

1 cup milk	2 whole eggs, at room
12 rose-scented geranium	temperature
leaves	2¾ cups flour
1 cup unsalted butter,	2 teaspoons baking powder
softened	½ teaspoon salt
1½ cups sugar	1 teaspoon grated lemon
3 egg whites, at room	zest
temperature	1 teaspoon vanilla extract

1. About 30 minutes before preparing the cake batter, heat the milk in a small saucepan. Remove from the heat just before it begins to boil. Add six rose-scented geranium leaves. Cover and let cool to room temperature.
2. Preheat oven to 350°F. Grease and lightly flour two 8- or 9-inch cake pans.
3. Finely chop six rose-scented geranium leaves (to make 2 tablespoons), and sprinkle on the bottom of both cake pans.
4. Cream the butter and sugar. Beat in the egg whites and then the whole eggs.
5. Mix the dry ingredients and lemon zest in a small bowl.
6. Strain the leaves from the milk and discard them. Add the vanilla to the strained milk.

7. Add the dry ingredients to the egg mixture, alternating with the milk mixture.
8. Pour the batter into the prepared pans. Bake 25 to 30 minutes, or until layers test done. Remove from the pans after cooling slightly. Cool the layers to room temperature before icing and assembling.

Melba Sauce

Serve a Melba Sauce made with ruby-red raspberries over vanilla ice cream as an accompaniment to Rose-Scented Geranium Valentine's Day Cake. Make the sauce while the cake is baking, so that it can chill in the refrigerator until serving time. Be sure to reserve 1 or 2 teaspoons of the raspberry syrup to tint and flavor the Cream Cheese Icing for the cake.

> 1 cup canned peaches, including ¼ cup syrup
> 1 box (8 ounces) frozen red raspberries, thawed
> 1 tablespoon lemon juice

Puree the peaches, raspberries, and lemon juice in a blender or food processor. Chill until serving time.

Cream Cheese Icing

This recipe makes enough icing for the sides and top of a layer cake. Between the layers, I like to use rose-scented geranium jelly (see page 20), or you can use raspberry or other fruit jam.

> 4 tablespoons (½ stick) unsalted butter, softened
> 4 ounces cream cheese, softened
> 2 cups confectioners' sugar
> 1–2 teaspoons frozen raspberry syrup (reserved from the frozen raspberries in the Melba Sauce, above)

1. Beat all the ingredients with an electric mixer until soft and creamy. Add enough raspberry syrup to make a spreadable icing.
2. Spread on sides and top of the cooled cake.

Chai

MAKES 4 CUPS

Chai is a fragrant, Indian-style tea. Holy basil is the secret ingredient in this recipe, but any basil is good in chai. For best results, use a strong black tea such as Assam or Darjeeling.

 1 cup milk (either low-fat or soy)
 3 cups water
 3 cardamom pods, coarsely crushed
 3–4 whole cloves
 1 cinnamon stick (1 inch)
 1–3 black peppercorns, coarsely crushed
 3–4 teaspoons loose black tea
 4–6 sprigs holy basil (or 1 frozen cube, see page 116)
   Freshly grated nutmeg, for garnish

Heat milk, water, cardamom, cloves, cinnamon sticks, and peppercorns in a saucepan over medium heat. When mixture is just ready to boil, remove from heat; add tea and holy basil. Cover and let sit 5 minutes. Strain, and serve topped with the grated nutmeg.

Pine-Needle Tea

After the garden is blackened by frost and you're longing for something freshly picked, gather fragrant pine needles for afternoon tea. A handful (24 to 30 needles) is all you need. Bring 4 cups of water to a boil, and pour over the snipped pine needles. Cover the pot and steep 5 to 10 minutes. Strain and serve the mildly resinous tea warm, with honey and lemon if desired. Believe it or not, pine needles have a significant amount of vitamin C!

Safety first: Do not use the needles from your Christmas tree if purchased or soaked in preservative-treated water. Preservatives sprayed on Christmas trees and added to the water in the tree stand are extremely toxic. Take special care to protect young children and pets from this hazard, as well.

CHAPTER 6

GROWING, PRESERVING, AND
Using Herbs

I f I had space for only the tiniest garden, herbs are the plants I would choose to grow. There's something sacred and timeless about herbs. Because the parsley, sage, rosemary, and thyme we grow today are descendants of the very plants the ancient Greeks and Romans used, just breathing their fragrance makes me feel connected to countless generations who have shared the same simple delight. Along with this link to the past, herbs provide many opportunities to take charge of life, create pleasures, and satisfy personal needs. The pungent flavor of fresh basil, the soothing comfort of a cup of chamomile tea, and the physical delight of digging in the earth can be grounding and strengthening. May the generosity of the good earth and the green growing plants fill your heart as well.

95

WHERE TO GROW HERBS

Happily, herbs are among the easiest plants to grow. Given enough sunlight and good drainage, herbs will grow in almost any type of soil, and most can withstand long periods of drought. And because of their aromatic nature, most herbs seem to repel destructive insects and hungry wildlife, too.

If your site is boggy or densely shaded, give container growing a try. (For advice about growing herbs in containers, see page 105.) Because planters heat up and drain faster than in-ground plantings, many herbs that sulk in cool, damp conditions will grow happily in pots. And a few herbs actually prefer partial shade over full sun. These include angelica, chervil, cilantro, comfrey, lemon balm, mints, sweet cicely, sweet woodruff, and violets. A few sun-preferring herbs will also adapt to partial shade, especially once the weather warms up. Try situating borage, burnet, dill, fennel, hyssop, parsley, and sage in light shade.

You don't need a separate garden for your herbs. Although most herbs aren't typically grown for their blossoms, most have attractive shapes and foliage, so they combine beautifully with flowering plants and shrubs. Tuck annual herbs like basil, dill, and marjoram into flower

---

Ideal Site for a Culinary Herb Garden

Although herbs are remarkably resilient and adaptable, you will have the greatest success with most herbs if you give them a spot with the following conditions:

- Full sun at least 6 hours a day
- Well-drained (no long-lasting puddles when it rains)
- Conveniently located to the hose and the kitchen
- Limited competition from large trees that draw water and nutrients

- Protected from marauding pets and children's play areas
- Located away from underground utility lines and the septic tank or other water and sewer lines
- Relatively flat site

beds and vegetable gardens. Perennial herbs like sage, lovage, and thyme will be right at home in established flower beds, and they're good partners for asparagus and rhubarb in a perennial vegetable patch.

LAYING THE GROUNDWORK

Creating a design is the first step in establishing a new garden site. Gather ideas from other gardens and gardening books and magazines. Rectangles and squares are usually the easiest shapes to work with, but if the site or your heart begs for something different, follow your inspiration. I never plant in straight lines, even though my artistic notions usually create more challenging spaces to maintain.

To preview your garden layout, outline the perimeter with a hose or rope. Spread newspaper to mark the bed. Stand back and imagine what you'd like to plant where. Before going inside, mark the bed with stakes and sketch your ideas on paper. Later, spend time plotting herb placement, taking into consideration ultimate size, shape, and color, as well as seasonal factors like early- and late-season crops.

Edible Knot Gardens

Traditionally worked in perennial herbs like lavender and germander, knot gardens are stunning, but they can be an expensive and time-consuming investment. Here's a cheaper option, especially if you start plants from seed: Use basils! For a formal look, select a compact basil such as basil 'Finissimo Verde' or 'Spicy Globe'. Make a color splash and interplant 'Dark Opal' basil with a green-leafed form. A bonus beyond the aesthetic appeal of this garden: You can eat the results!

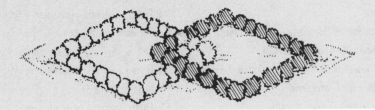

SALAD GARDEN

Create a complete salad garden using recycled wooden crates, or build your own boxes from wood scraps. For longer life, treat the wood with boiled linseed oil. (Do not use pressure-treated wood, as the chemicals that kill rot, which are living organisms, can also kill plants.) Lining the wood with heavy-duty plastic also helps retard rot. Be sure to punch drainage holes in the plastic. If you take both of these preventive measures, your salad garden containers should hold up for five to seven years. I like to intermingle edible flowers (calendula and Johnny-jump-ups) and greens, such as arugula and several varieties of lettuce, with salad herbs in this decorative mini-garden. Follow the advice on growing herbs in containers, The Potted Herb, beginning on page 105.

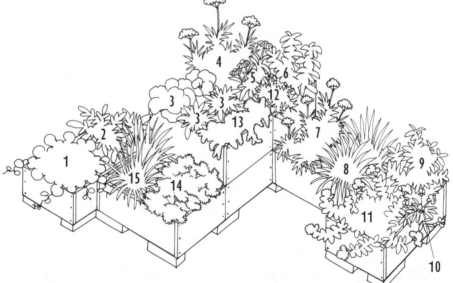

1. Nasturtium *(Tropaeolum majus)*
2. Arugula *(Eruca sativa)*
3. Lettuce
4. Bronze fennel *(Foeniculum vulgare 'Bronze')*
5. Calendula *(Calendula officinalis)*
6. Lettuce-leaf basil *(Ocimum basilicum 'Crispum')*
7. Dill *(Anethum graveolens)*
8. Garlic chives *(Allium tuberosum)*
9. Lemon basil *(Ocimum basilicum 'Citriodorum')*
10. Johnny-jump-ups *(Viola tricolor)*
11. Sweet marjoram *(Origanum majorana)*
12. Summer savory *(Satureja hortensis)*
13. Lemon thyme *(Thymus serpyllum 'Citriodorus')*
14. Italian parsley *(Petroselinum crispum var. neapolitanum)*
15. Chives *(Allium schoenoprasum)*

SALSA GARDEN

Here's enough spicy heat to keep salsa lovers in tears all summer! For tomato-based dips that don't drip, choose meaty, small-fruited tomato varieties such as red 'Roma' and 'Juliet', and yellow 'Wonder Light' and 'Yellow Bell'. Other colorful salsa tomatoes include medium-size golden types like 'Djena Lee' and 'Golden Jubilee'; 'Eva Purple' is a variety with beautiful pink-purple fruit. Tomatillos are 1- to 2-inch green fruits that grow within a thin husk. They like the same treatment you'd give tomatoes, including sun and heat; they don't need staking. Be sure to plant only one quillquina: this plant can grow 4 to 5 feet tall. By the way, please *do* eat the flowers in this design. Mexican roses are kissing cousins to the potherb purslane (*Portulaca oleracea*). Both flowers and leaves are edible.

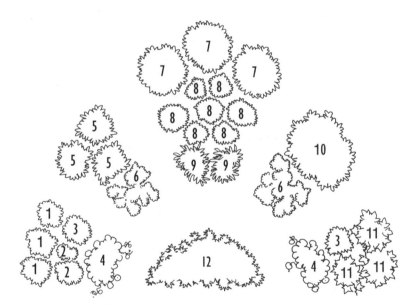

1. Tomatillos
2. Cinnamon basil (*Ocimum basilicum* 'Cinnamon')
3. Jalapeño peppers
4. Nasturtiums (*Tropaeolum majus*)
5. Bell pepper
6. Cilantro (*Coriandrum sativum*)
7. Tomatoes
8. Basil (*Ocimum basilicum*)
9. Calendula (*Calendula officinalis*)
10. Quillquina (*Porophyllum ruderale*)
11. Cucumbers
12. Mexican roses (*Portulaca grandiflora*)

SPAGHETTI OR PIZZA GARDEN

Here's a summer garden loaded with the makings for pasta sauces and pizza toppings. For thick sauces, choose meaty small and medium-size tomatoes (see page 99 for variety names). 'Anaheim' and 'Ancho' are flavorful pepper varieties; jalapeños offer comfortable heat. For a sweeter pepper, try 'Sweet Chocolate'. And for heat lovers, habañero peppers (especially 'Red Savina') hit the top of the Scovill heat-rating scale for fire! For healthy green pizza toppings, grow a patch of mixed greens, such as chard, arugula, and chicory. Use nasturtium and calendula petals as colorful, decorative accents when you serve.

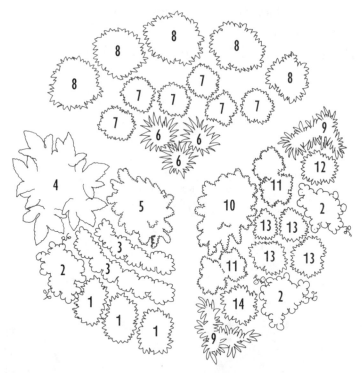

1. Jalapeño peppers
2. Nasturtiums *(Tropaeolum majus)*
3. Mixed greens
4. Zucchini
5. Oregano *(Origanum vulgare)*
6. Garlic chives *(Allium tuberosum)*
7. Basil *(Ocimum basilicum 'Genovese')*
8. Tomatoes

9. Calendula *(Calendula officinalis)*
10. Sweet marjoram *(Origanum majorana)*
11. Italian parsley *(Petroselinum crispum var. neapolitanum)*
12. Anaheim pepper
13. Bell pepper
14. Ancho pepper

A Seed-Saver's Herb Garden

Seed saving is a wonderful way to furnish your own garden, help other gardeners, and ensure seeds for future generations. Let's say you have several wonderful plants of lemon basil. In late summer, allow some of the plants to flower, then wither until dark stalks develop where the flowers were. Before the frost comes, clip off the entire seed stalk, and place it in a paper bag, which will catch any seeds that might fall out.

When you have time, spread some white paper on a work table and empty the stalks on the paper. You'll probably see some tiny black seeds among the brown chaff. Pick those out and place them in a paper envelope. To find the remaining seeds, strip the seed capsules from the flower stalks and place them in a wire mesh strainer. Rub the plant material against the mesh to release more seeds. If there's a lot of chaff mixed in with the seeds, blow lightly to dispel the debris. Once you've gathered all the seeds, close the envelope and label it with the type of seed and the year harvested. Most seeds will remain viable for three to five years if stored in a cool, dry place, but dill, cilantro, fennel, and other herbs in the carrot family are best planted within a year after harvesting.

Lemon basil seed stalk

Remove chaff by pressing plant material against strainer.

In addition to sharing seeds within your local community, consider joining the Seed Savers Exchange, a national nonprofit organization committed to preserving biodiversity. SSE focuses on vegetables, fruits, and grains, whereas a sister network, the Flower and Herb Exchange, is devoted exclusively to flowers and herbs. (See Herbal Resources for address.)

Digging In

Once you've determined where to plant, you can prepare the soil. My favorite method requires very little digging. Begin by mowing the site, using the lowest setting on the mower. (If your soil is clay, till the soil after mowing.) To suffocate the grass, spread newspaper at least eight pages thick over the mowed area. Keep the newspaper in place and prevent it from wicking moisture from the soil by soaking it with water, then covering it with at least 2 inches of compost, topsoil, or a good soil mix. Add a balanced organic fertilizer at the rate listed on the package. Add lime only if a soil test indicates that you need it. Rake the bed smooth, then sprinkle it with water until it's evenly moist. When the weather is right (see specific herbs in Chapter 7, beginning on page 123), set in your plants, cutting right through the newspaper with a trowel to make the planting holes. This method works even better if the site is prepared the autumn previous to spring planting.

If you want good soil in a hurry, consider purchasing a load of topsoil and spreading it on top of the newspaper to a depth of 6 to 8 inches. Be sure to investigate the quality of the soil before it's dumped in your yard. I buy a product that's half composted leaves and half topsoil. Having soil that's easy to dig in makes every garden activity a breeze.

Use a trowel to cut through soil, layers of newspaper, and sod.

Seeds and Transplants

Once you've created a place to plant, select five herbs you already know you like and one or two you'd like to learn about. For many herbs, one plant of each variety is enough for the average family, but you may want two or three plants of frequently used annual herbs, such as basil, dill, and cilantro. If you plan to make lots of pesto or brew herb vinegars, you'll need at least a dozen plants of each.

When choosing herbs and planning where you will make homes for them, it's helpful to understand that plants have different types of life cycles.

Hardy annuals. Annuals are plants that complete their growth cycle (grow, flower, set seed, and die) in one growing season. Some favorite hardy annual herbs are borage, calendula, chervil, cilantro, and dill. Of these, chervil, cilantro, and dill grow best from seed sown at the cooler ends of the growing season. To get a head start, sow them in late fall where you want plants to grow; they'll sprout the following spring. Or, sow them several weeks before the last frost in the spring. Either way you'll be able to harvest them until summer heats up.

Warm-weather or tender annuals. Wait until frosts are behind you before planting basils, nasturtiums, and summer savory. It's easy to start these annuals from seed in warm soil if you remember to keep the area moist until plants emerge, or purchase one or two transplants.

Perennials. Perennials can be divided into two groups: hardy perennials, like lavender, mint, sage, and thyme, which tolerate freezing conditions; and tender perennials, such as bay, scented-leaf geraniums, lemongrass, rosemary, and lemon verbena, which don't. Consult Chapter 7, starting on page 123, or a garden encyclopedia for advice on the hardiness range of the perennial herbs you'd like to grow. (Hardiness zones indicate the average annual minimum temperatures of various regions of North America. Check with your local nursery to find out your area's hardiness zone.)

Many hardy perennial herbs are easy to grow. For quickest results, start with purchased transplants or cuttings from a friend, as perennials grown from seed often take two seasons to develop into mature plants. Plant hardy perennials in early to late spring, so they will have time to get well established before the weather gets hot.

Unless you live in Zone 9 or 10, it's best to grow tender perennials in pots that can be brought indoors at summer's end. You can sink the pots in the ground, so that you can remove the plant, pot and all, without disturbing its roots, or enjoy it as a container plant on the porch or deck outdoors in summer, and bring it in for winter.

GROWING-SEASON CARE

Most in-ground herbs need little care once planted. If Mother Nature doesn't provide, water new transplants every day or two until the rain fills in. Once herbs are off and growing, they aren't likely to require supplemental water unless drought becomes severe. I add seaweed solution to the water (2 tablespoons solution per gallon of water) when I put in new herb plants, but that's typically the extent of any fertilizing program. However, if you have a small garden and harvest regularly, you may want faster growth. In that case, foliar feed every three weeks. (See page 107.)

Mulch. Good mulches for herbs are shredded leaves, dried grass clippings, or straw. Do not use heavy wood chips, especially if you are growing lavender or other herbs that dislike acidity. These mulches not only pack down and suffocate roots, but wood chips, as well as pine needles and oak leaves, are also very acidic.

Pruning. Regular trimming keeps growth more tender and sweet. Every two weeks, walk through your garden with pruners or scissors in hand, and snip off unwanted buds, trim back leggy growth, and cut off any weak-looking branches. Remove as much as a third of the plant if necessary.

Prune plants regularly, and use clippings in your cooking.

Winter care. In early winter, cover hardy perennials like lavender, sage, and thyme with a light mulch. The mulch keeps the soil from alternately freezing and thawing, which is the biggest cause of winterkill where snow cover is not reliable. Evergreen branches placed loosely around the base of the plants are perfect for this purpose. (Remember to remove the branches in the spring, so that they don't add acidity to the soil.) If you live in an area where you can count on a deep snow cover, there's no need to mulch, because nature's winter blanket will do the job.

THE POTTED HERB

Do you have problem soil, no time to prepare soil, too much shade, or no garden soil at all? If you answered yes to any of these questions, container gardening may be the answer for you. Most herbs make ideal container plants, and pots can be located close to the house and situated so that little bending is required.

MATERIAL MATTERS

Keeping your plants moist is the primary challenge of container gardening. Larger containers need less frequent watering, so you can save yourself time by planting several plants in one large container. Determine what size container to use by the number of plants: Four transplants from 4-inch pots fit well in a 10-inch container. Wooden containers, such as half-whiskey barrels, retain moisture and "breathe," so soil stays cooler during hot spells. Airtight plastic pots also retain moisture, but black plastic absorbs heat from the sun and can virtually bake plants. Clay pots are so porous that moisture quickly wicks away.

Drill plenty of holes in the bottom of all containers for drainage. To improve drainage further and to protect containers and the surface where they sit from rot, place them on bricks or blocks. Beyond these considerations, the choice of containers depends mostly on aesthetics and cost. Besides half-whiskey barrels, I also like to recycle found objects, such as dresser drawers, old wagons, and wooden crates.

Herbs by the Bushel

Bushel baskets are another inexpensive option. Simply line a basket with a plastic trash bag, slash a few holes in the plastic for drainage, and fill it with a good soil mix (see page 106). Placed on bricks, these gardens-to-go — complete with handles — will last all season.

SOIL FOR CONTAINERS

It takes a lot of soil mix to fill large containers, but you don't have to use 100 percent soil. Fill the bottom half of deep containers like half-whiskey barrels with twigs, leaves, or pinecones. Or, use Styrofoam peanuts or aluminum soda cans turned upside down, which have the added advantage of making large containers lighter and therefore easier to move around. Don't fill containers with garden soil; it's just too heavy. A good recipe for a container mix for herbs is equal parts purchased potting soil, sand, and compost. For best results, add granulated organic fertilizer according to package recommendations.

WATER WISELY

Containers dry out much more quickly than in-ground plantings do. Most planters need watering at least every other day during hot summer months. Be sure to place saucers underneath pots to hold extra water, but remember to empty them when there's a rainy spell so the plants don't get waterlogged. Mulching the soil in containers also helps. I use a 2-inch layer of shredded leaves with good success.

Automated Watering

If you will be away frequently and have no one to water in your absence, consider investing in an automatic irrigation system, with spigots that deliver water to each container on a schedule you can program.

vinyl tubing

hose

dripper

FEEDING POTTED HERBS

Herbs planted in the garden generally need very little fertilizer, but life in containers is different. Every time you water, liquid leaches through the container and flushes out water-soluble nutrients as it goes. Every three to four weeks, I feed all my container plants with a seaweed solution applied to their leaves, using 1 tablespoon seaweed solution per gallon of water in a pump-type sprayer. Called foliar feeding, this is a great supplemental feeding technique, as plants can absorb nutrients much faster through their leaves than through their roots. For best results, foliar feed in the early morning or early evening when the pores of the leaves are open to absorb dew. Use the finest mist setting on the sprayer, and mist both the tops and undersides of the leaves.

Five-Herb Medley

Select five favorite herbs to grow in pots, and place them near your kitchen door, so you're more likely to use them. Here are some great ideas to build an herbal palette that suits your family and your cooking style!

Mediterranean Medley: basil, marjoram, parsley, rosemary, thyme

A Taste of Provence: chervil, chives, lavender, tarragon, thyme

Lemon Lovers: lemon balm, lemon basil, lemon thyme, lemon verbena, lemongrass

Snappy Salsa: basil, cilantro, papalo, parsley, spearmint — and some jalapeño peppers!

Herb Vinegars: burnet, mint, opal basil, rosemary, tarragon

Thyme for Tea: anise hyssop, chamomile, lemon balm, lemon verbena, spearmint

Herbs for Kids: opal basil, Peter Rabbit's chamomile, bronze fennel, chocolate mint, nasturtium

Tina's Favorites: sweet basil, garlic chives, marjoram, Italian parsley, rosemary — Help! Can't stop! — holy basil, lavender, blue balsam mint, sage, summer savory, lemon thyme, and more

All in Good Thyme:
An Herb Garden Calendar

Over the years, I've developed a calendar that helps me remember successful garden strategies. This is a rough schedule for my Maryland herb garden, where the average last frost date is May 10–18 and the average first frost is October 10. To adjust for your hardiness zone, compare the dates listed for your zone and subtract or add the number of weeks' difference. To make it easier to create your own herb garden calendar, take photographs throughout the season to document your garden. And keep a written record, so that you can develop a schedule that works for you. Most of all, enjoy being in your garden, drinking in the beauty of life!

January. Use evergreen boughs, such as branches from a discarded Christmas tree, to mulch lavender, sage, thyme, tarragon, and other perennial herbs subject to frost heave. Harvest pine needles for tea (see page 94). Order seed catalogs, read garden books and magazines, take lots of herbal baths, and dream about your garden.

February. Bring dream gardens to earth on paper. Order seeds and other materials. Host an herb seed swap and sample herbal teas. Repair garden tools. Make sure mulch stays in place. Begin pruning evergreen herbs (lavender, sage, thyme) on mild days. Harvest chickweed, garlic mustard, and wintercress. If your soil is acidic, spread lime over receding snow.

March. Rake mulch from beds and sow seeds of hardy annual herbs, like calendula, chervil, cilantro, dill, nigella, and poppies. Harvest early spring potherbs like dandelions and violets. Listen for those first signs of spring: spring peepers, returning geese, and robins.

April. Divide perennial herbs. Take cuttings. Plant new perennials. If you've started plants indoors, transplant hardy annual seedlings. Sow basil, nasturtium, and savory seeds indoors. Finish pruning herbs. Prepare any new garden areas when the soil warms. Renew established gardens with compost and leaf mold. Dye Easter eggs with natural dyes (see page 34). Harvest dandelions, nettles, and other spring wildings. Make a fresh batch of potting soil.

May. Make May Day baskets brimming with herbs and spring flowers. Begin hardening off indoor plants like bay, scented geraniums, and rosemary, as well as seedlings started indoors. Complete preparation of garden beds and containers. Plant annuals when the ground is warm and dry enough to cultivate and frost no longer threatens. Mulch garden pathways. Lie in the grass and watch clouds skip across the sky.

June. Add final touches to the garden, keeping transplants well watered. Keep up with the weeds, mulching if necessary. Harvest and preserve early-spring herbs — calendula, chervil, cilantro, red clover blossoms, dandelions, and nettles. Dance in the moonlight on Midsummer Eve. Celebrate the solstice.

July. Keep herbs and flowers trimmed. Plant a second crop of basil and summer savory if these plants have gone to seed. Begin preserving herbs. Watch the butterflies. Nap in the shade.

August. Early in the month, prune summer herbs by one-third to one-half, and foliar feed to encourage new growth. Sow seeds of hardy annuals (calendula, chervil, cilantro, dill, parsley) and biennials (angelica, caraway), and sow a new crop of salad greens. Take cuttings of basils and scented geraniums for indoor plants. If tender perennials aren't potted, dig them up, cut them back, and keep them in partial shade until bringing indoors before the first frost. Make and freeze pesto. Make herb vinegars. Begin drying herbs. Say good-bye to the hummingbirds. Watch the shadows lengthen.

September. Plant saffron crocus and garlic. Last call for freezing basil. Harvest remaining summer herbs before the first frost. Bring tender perennials indoors. Save seeds. Make Rosemary-Goldenrod Jelly (page 22), herb mustards, herb butters, and other pantry staples. Watch for a new crop of chickweed, dandelions, and nettles.

October. Clean up the garden, clipping off dead foliage at ground level and composting it. Prepare new garden beds. Mulch leaves. Carve pumpkins. Make dried wreaths. Wave to the geese.

November. Finish any remaining garden cleanup. Make notes for next year while you can remember! Give thanks for the bounty of the earth.

December. Prepare holiday gifts. Celebrate the winter solstice!

HERBS ANYTHYME: THE INDOOR HERB GARDEN

Most herbs need strong sunlight to thrive and thus are challenging houseplants, especially during the dark days of winter. But you can enjoy many fresh herbs, and overwinter others, with little extra effort.

In early fall, I gather potted bay, scented geranium, and rosemary plants and set them on an outdoor porch so they'll get accustomed to less light. When frost threatens, I put the rosemaries and as many other plants as I can fit in the sunniest windows in the house. I water the plants twice a week, adding seaweed solution to the water to make life indoors bearable. I also mist the plants once or twice a week to keep up the humidity. Cooler temperatures (55 to 65°F) are ideal. The plants I don't have room for go down to the basement, where it's cool. Because there's not enough light for the plants to flourish, I encourage them to become semi-dormant by watering them only about once every three weeks.

Mist indoor plants weekly.

In late March or early April, I trim all the plants, including those that are semi-dormant, repot those whose roots are cramped and need bigger pots, add compost to the pots, and put them in a sheltered spot outdoors when frost is no longer likely. Once weather is dependably mild, I gradually accustom them to outdoor sunlight.

Using this method, scented geraniums grow well for two or three seasons, and rosemary, for four or five years. The bay just keeps going, and the biggest problem I face with it is moving such a large plant!

SUMMER HERBS IN DEEPEST WINTER

If you want to grow summer herbs indoors for more than occasional winter use, you'll find that even your sunniest window doesn't provide enough light for robust growth. For successful indoor herb growing, invest in fluorescent light fixtures. Regular shop lights that hold four tubes provide enough growing area for most families. A mixture of cool white and warm white tubes works well. Hang the light fixture so that you can adjust its height. Position the lights so they are only 6 to 8 inches above plants. (You'll need to raise them as plants grow.) Buy a timer that will turn the lights on and off automatically, and set it for 16 hours on and 8 hours off. This setup is good for starting seeds.

HARVESTING AND STORING HERBS

When is the best time to harvest herbs? The short answer is: Whenever you need them! But if you can wait, or you're harvesting a large number of herbs for storage, the ideal time is just after the morning dew has evaporated or when it cools off in the evening. New gardeners are often timid about cutting herbs, but regular harvesting actually encourages growth. Each week, harvest a little extra to dry or freeze or make herbal vinegars and jellies. You can vigorously cut back growing plants by one-third to two-thirds of their height without stunting growth. Harvest all annuals completely before the first frost.

Cutting tools. Invest in at least one pair of sharp culinary scissors. They make fast work of cutting both woody and tender stalks without straining your wrists or crushing plants. For clipping tiny chamomile flower heads or tender dill fronds, a pair of small "blossom-size" scissors are ideal. Both pairs are useful for mincing herbs in the kitchen as well.

Culinary and flower cutting scissors

Harvest basket. Treat yourself to a roomy basket to gather herbs. Line the basket with a pretty tea towel if you like. A flat-bottomed basket will accommodate a few berry baskets to separate herbs, or a plastic container of water to refresh stems if you'll be out in the sun for a while. You can also make layers of different herbs, using damp tea towels to separate them.

Harvest basket

THE WHEN AND HOW
OF HARVESTING

Leaves. Begin clipping the tender
tops when plants are 3 inches tall. On
upright, branching plants like basil and
rosemary, cut just above a node, which is
the spin-off point for new growth. As the
plants bush out, trim the branching stems
in the same manner (see illustration, page
104). For sprawling plants like marjoram and thyme, gather a few sprigs
between your fingers and snip them
en masse. For clump-forming
plants like chives, dill, and parsley,
clip off a few stalks at ground level.

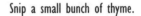

Snip a small bunch of thyme.

Clip a few outer stems
of parsley.

Flowers. Harvest flowers when they
first open or a little earlier, that is, when
the bud just begins to show color. Remove flowers with enough stem
to place in water, or just above the next blossom in line to bloom.

Seeds. Cut seed heads as they begin to turn brown but before they
shatter (that point at which the seeds fall out of the seedpods).
Because seeds ripen unevenly, it's usually safer to finish drying them
by hanging the seed heads upside down in a brown paper bag tied off
at the top. Be sure to punch a few holes in the sides of the bag to
allow for air circulation.

CARE OF THE HARVEST

There's no need to wash herbs unless
they are visibly dirty. Store herbs for short-
term use in a glass of water. First, crush
their stems slightly with a wooden
spoon. If you're keeping them for
more than a day or two, place the
glass in a plastic bag, close with a

Place herb stems in
a glass of water, and
store in a plastic bag.

twist tie, and refrigerate. Or wrap cuttings in a damp towel and enclose them in a plastic bag. Close the bag only loosely. Check herbs every other day and remoisten the towel if necessary.

DRYING HERBS FOR WINTER USE

The best time to harvest leafy herbs is just before full flowering, when they're in their prime. Select a sunny day during a dry spell. If the herbs are dirty, rinse them with the hose the night before, so you won't need to wet them again. As soon as possible after harvesting, proceed with one of the following drying methods:

Hang drying. Lay stalks on a counter and sort them by size. Bunch together three to five stem ends and tie tightly with rubber bands, twist ties, or damp twine. (Damp twine shrinks slightly when dry, creating a tighter knot.) If you use twine, cut a piece about 18 inches long, and tie a bunch of herbs on each end. Hang the herbs in an area with good air circulation but out of direct sunlight, which causes fading. String a clothesline in a vacant space or use a clothes-drying rack, and hang bunches of herbs with clothespins. If you don't have a suitable space that's out of direct sunlight, bunch the herbs in paper bags with the stem ends coming out of the top of the bag. Punch several holes in the bag to allow for air circulation. Remember, you have to let out the moisture!

Tie an herb bundle to each end of a piece of twine.

Screen drying. Place a screen on wood blocks, and lay herbs in a single layer on the screen. You can continue stacking wood blocks and additional screens on top to save space while accomodating more herbs.

Mechanical dryers. Follow the manufacturer's instructions for drying herbs with a food dehydrator or microwave.

"Hot box." On a hot, sunny morning, line the seats and floor of your car with newspaper. Lay herbs in a single layer on the paper and then cover with another layer of paper so that the herbs don't fade. Open the windows a bit to allow moisture to escape. By the end of the day, herbs should be ready to store.

Dried Herbs Fresh from the Fridge

Herbs with a lot of water in their leaves, such as basil, dill, and parsley, lose flavor when hang-dried. Here's a better way to preserve them: If you've rinsed your herbs, gently pat them dry with a clean towel and let them air until no moisture is left on the leaves. Place several stems in a single layer in a brown paper bag. Place the bag in a frost-free refrigerator and tape to the side. Within a week, the herbs will be dried, and you can store as for other dried herbs. The defrosting mechanism, which is designed to remove moist air from the refrigerator, draws the moisture from the herbs. Plus, there's no light to discolor the leaves, and the cool temperature preserves flavor.

STORING DRIED HERBS

Although it's pleasant to see herbs hanging from the kitchen ceiling, this exposure to moisture in the air quickly degrades their flavor. Reserve some bunches for decoration if you like, but store those you'll cook with as soon as the leaves are crackly dry. Unless you live in an arid climate, it's wise to "finish off" hang-dried herbs with a brief stint in the oven. Strip the leaves from the stems, taking care not to crumble the leaves more than necessary, as that would release essential oils before you can capture them in foods. Spread leaves in a single layer on a baking sheet. Preheat oven to 120°F, and place the baking sheet in the oven for five minutes. Remove and allow herbs to cool to room temperature. Store the leaves in airtight containers. Most cooks prefer to use glass or ceramic containers, as metal or plastic can affect the flavor of delicate herbs. Be sure to label the containers, not only with the name of the herb but also with the date. Store the containers in a cool, dark cupboard (not over the stove!) for up to a year.

To use home-dried herbs in recipes, crumble the leaves when measuring to get an accurate count, then proceed as directed.

A Gift of Herbs

Home-dried herbs are welcome gifts. Package single herbs or formulate your own herbal blends (see pages 9–13 for suggestions). Decorative labels will beautify this special gift:

- Cut pictures from seed catalogs or magazines and paste them to jars with a glue stick.
- Buy blank labels and print them with herb stamps by inking a sprig of the herb with a sponge ink pad and pressing it onto the label.

FREEZING HERBS FOR FRESH FLAVOR

Many chefs are discovering that frozen herbs have big flavor advantages. Herbs like chervil, chives, and cilantro, for example, are virtually tasteless when dried. Other herbs, like sage, become more harshly flavored. Moisture-filled herbs like basil and parsley are troublesome to dry without mechanical assistance.

If you freeze your herbs, on the other hand, you can capture fresh-picked flavor. Because the texture becomes mushy and the color darker, frozen herbs are best when you add them to cooked dishes like soups, stews, and sauces. Frozen herbs retain good flavor for two to four months.

You have a choice of several methods of freezing herbs:

Pack and freeze. For the least amount of fuss, simply pack herbs in freezer bags. If the stalks are tough, strip the leaves from the stems first. Label and date the bags and freeze.

Blanch and freeze. Some chefs find that blanching fresh herbs improves keeping power, especially with herbs like basil and lovage. Using tongs to hold the stem ends of the herbs, dip them in boiling water for 5 to 10 seconds, lift out, and sponge lightly between cotton towels to dry or whirl in a salad spinner. Place herbs in a self-sealing plastic freezer bag, then dip the bag in a bowl of cold water, being careful not to allow water into the opening. Press the bag to force out excess air, and seal. To use herbs frozen in this manner, break or slice off what you need and drop into soup or spaghetti sauce. Measure as for fresh herbs: two to three times the amount specified for dried herbs.

Puree and freeze. Another easy way to freeze herbs is to puree them in a blender, adding just enough water to make a slurry. Freeze the mixture in ice cube trays or plastic containers like recycled yogurt cups (note that pureed herbs will stain plastic ice cube trays). When the slurry is frozen, pop it out of the container and store in a labeled freezer bag. To use, drop a frozen cube into sauces, casseroles, or soup. If the additional water poses a problem with a recipe, thaw first, and strain out excess water.

Herb pastes. If you don't mind adding oil to a recipe, freezing herb pastes is an excellent way to retain fresh flavor. To make a paste, puree herbs, adding just enough vegetable oil to reduce herbs to a smooth paste — about ½ cup oil to 2 cups packed fresh herb leaves. It's easier to use a food processor to puree, but a blender will work if you stop the motor periodically and push the mixture down with a rubber spatula. Some cooks prefer to use extra-virgin olive oil to make herb pastes, especially if they plan to use the paste as a start to making pesto. If you're not sure how you'll be using the paste, however, use canola or sunflower oil, as either one adds less of its own flavor to the herb paste. Pack the herb paste in airtight, freezer-safe containers, such as yogurt containers. Label and date them. Freeze the paste immediately to avoid contamination.

Herb pastes are very convenient to use in any recipe calling for dried herbs, as the mixture doesn't freeze solid. Simply scoop out what you need with a spoon. Because the flavor is more concentrated, measure one-third to one-half less herb paste than the amount specified for dried herbs.

Safety first. The combination of oil and fresh plant materials creates an environment that encourages the growth of bacteria. Use herb pastes immediately or keep them frozen.

HERBAL VINEGARS

Before refrigeration was available, many herbs were preserved in wine or vinegar. Today, herbal vinegars are a popular way to add flavor to salad dressings, mustards, marinades, soups, and casseroles, as well as to spike the cooking water for pasta or rice without adding fat, sugar, or salt. The vinegars have dozens of household uses, as well (see Practical Herbal Vinegars, below). Herbal vinegars are easy to create from fresh home-grown herbs, and they also make great gifts.

Once you've tried the basic recipe, have fun experimenting with various herbs, singly or in combination, as well as with different types of vinegar. White wine and rice vinegars are ideal for preserving the lovely color of opal basil leaves, chive blossoms, nasturtium flowers, and other bright herbs. They're also mild enough to retain the delicate flavor of burnet, dill, and tarragon. Red wine and apple cider vinegars stand up to more strongly flavored herbs, like rosemary. Most chefs avoid distilled white vinegar, a coarse-tasting brew made from grain, petroleum by-products, or wood pulp.

Practical Herbal Vinegars

Using apple cider vinegar, you can brew up an all-purpose herb vinegar with mixed herb trimmings. Follow the basic recipe on page 118 and use your vinegars for any of the following household purposes:

- To clean wood floors, use 1 cup per gallon of warm water.
- For fresh-smelling towels and sheets, add 2 to 3 cups per large laundry load in the final rinse cycle.
- For sparkling clean windows and mirrors, mix ¼ cup herbal vinegar with 1 tablespoon cornstarch and 2 cups water in a jar with a tight, non-metal lid. Shake to dissolve cornstarch. Pour into a spray bottle to use.
- To ease tired muscles and leave skin feeling refreshed, add 2 to 4 cups to a full bathtub. (Don't worry, you won't smell like a pickle! The vinegar smell fades quickly.)

Basic Herbal Vinegar Recipe

YIELD: ½ GALLON

Present herbal vinegars in pretty bottles with a sprig or two of the featured herb floating in the brew. Make an herbal "necklace" for the bottle by stringing dried peppers with bay leaves, or embellish the bottle with a tiny grapevine wreath. Two proven herb-vinegar combinations are rosemary, shallots, and tarragon in red wine vinegar, and orange zest and spearmint in rice wine vinegar.

>   4 cups fresh herbs (not packed)
>   2 quarts vinegar

1. Place the fresh herbs in a clean glass jar. Cover them with vinegar.
2. Cap the jar using a nonmetal lid. (Metal sets up a reaction with the vinegar. You can purchase plastic lids made to fit standard jars in the canning section of most grocery or hardware stores.)
3. Let the jar sit in a cool, dark place for up to a month, or until it smells and tastes pleasantly flavored with the herb.
4. Strain out the plant material. If desired, filter once or twice through a coffee filter until the liquid is perfectly clear.
5. Pour the vinegar into a clean bottle, cork or cap tightly with a nonmetal lid, and label.

Use. For freshest flavor, use herbal vinegars within six months after opening.

Storage. Store flavored vinegars in a cool, dark place. Unopened, most vinegars will last at least a year or two.

Opal Basil-Garlic-Black Peppercorn Vinegar

Opal basil vinegar flavored with garlic and black peppercorns is my favorite herb vinegar combination. Make the basic recipe (above) using red or white wine vinegar, and add 2 teaspoons coarsely cracked black peppercorns and 6 to 8 garlic cloves, sliced.

HERBAL OILS

High in flavor but low in saturated fat and cholesterol, herb-flavored olive oils are the latest sizzle in gourmet skillets. Because oil is highly perishable once it is infused with plant material, make flavored oils in small batches and keep them refrigerated. Discard any leftovers after two weeks. Although dangerous spoilage is unlikely, bacteria that produce botulism can develop in the low acidity and airlessness conditions characteristic of oils. It's not worth taking a chance.

Basic Herb-Infused Oil Recipe

YIELD: 1 CUP

This basic recipe for a versatile infused oil is great for stir-fries or to brush on vegetables and meats before roasting, broiling, or grilling. Remember, you don't need to use much. A thin coating imparts rich flavor and keeps down the calories. Experiment with other fresh herbs. For stronger-flavored herbs, like lavender, rosemary, or thyme, use only ⅓ cup.

> 1 cup extra-virgin olive oil
> 3 cloves garlic, peeled and minced
> ½ cup basil leaves
> 1 teaspoon lemon juice or herb vinegar

1. Heat the olive oil in a skillet. When the oil is hot but not smoking, add the garlic and sauté, stirring frequently until the garlic barely begins to brown. Immediately remove from the heat.
2. Stir in basil and lemon juice or vinegar. Let sit for 1 hour at room temperature.
3. Strain the plant material and pour the oil into a sterilized bottle. For stronger flavored oil, you can leave in the herbs.
4. Cap the jar with a nonmetal lid, and label it, including the exact date.

Storage. Store the oil in the refrigerator. Discard any leftovers after two weeks. You'll find that olive oil congeals in the refrigerator. It's okay to let the oil stand at room temperature for an hour or so to let it clear before use, but keep it refrigerated otherwise.

Flavored Wine

Leftover wine? Instead of discarding it, pour it into a clean glass jar with a few sprigs of your favorite herbs. Use a scant ¼ cup of fresh herbs per cup of wine. Cap the jar tightly and refrigerate for at least a week before testing flavor. Herb-infused wine is great for marinades and sauces. For starters, try rosemary and garlic in red wine or lemon basil in white wine. Fruits and berries (¼ to ½ cup fruit per cup of wine) are also delicious combined with herbs. Happy experimenting!

SALTED HERBS

Salt has been used as a preservative since ancient times, and it is still a useful way to preserve savory herb leaves such as basil, lovage, marjoram, parsley, rosemary, sage, summer savory, tarragon, and thyme. The serendipitous result of this project is that you end up with two seasoning products: dried leaves and herb-flavored salt.

To make salted herbs, alternately layer even measures of fresh herb leaves (or tender sprigs) with sea salt in a wide-mouthed glass jar, starting and ending with a salt layer. Use a nonmetal lid to cap loosely, allowing the moisture to escape. Even taking this precaution, however, you'll find that the salt cakes a bit. Leaves will be dry in two to four weeks, depending on the moisture content of the herb.

To use the dried herbs, remove the leaves as needed. They are more potent than air-dried herbs; start with half as much as the recipe indicates.

You'll find that the salt used for drying is also pleasantly seasoned. For stronger herb flavor, grind some of the herbs into the salt. Used sparingly, herb salts are delightful for seasoning meats, roasted vegetables, and popcorn. And because herb salts are so full-flavored, you may be able to use less and decrease the amount of salt your family consumes.

HERBAL SUGARS AND SYRUPS

We've all but forgotten that sugar was once an important preservative. Today, herbal confections add an old-fashioned touch to a variety of desserts and drinks.

Herbal sugar. To make a subtle herb-flavored sugar to sweeten beverages or fresh fruits, or to bake into cakes and cookies, layer granulated sugar and herbs in a glass or food-quality plastic container, beginning and ending with a layer of sugar. To keep the sugar from clumping, stir every day or two. Remove the leaves before they crumble. Lavender buds, rose-scented geranium leaves, fragrant rose petals, and lemon verbena leaves are good candidates for this process.

Herbal syrup. Prepare a sugar syrup by boiling 3 cups of water and 2 cups of sugar in a nonaluminum saucepan. Stir in about 1 cup packed, fresh herb sprigs. Remove from heat and bring to room temperature. Remove herbs with tongs when they lose their color and the syrup is fragrant. Store in the refrigerator for up to three months. Use on pancakes, French toast, or waffles, or over fruit and ice cream. Try cinnamon basil, lemon balm, rose-scented geranium leaves, lavender, chocolate mint, rosemary, or lemon verbena. To make savory syrups for sauces and marinades, try basil, rosemary, sage, savory, tarragon, or thyme with a dash of citrus peel. Or, use the syrup to make an herb cooler: Pour ¼ cup herbal syrup over ice and add sparkling or mineral water. Garnish with fruit slices if desired. Popular flavors include anise hyssop, lemon balm, lavender, peppermint, rosemary, and spearmint.

Candied herbs. For a decorative touch, collect small edible flowers (violets, pansies, borage flowers, rose petals or buds, lavender sprigs) and herb leaves (mint, nasturtium, violet). Whisk 1 egg white with 2 teaspoons water until frothy, and brush on all flower and leaf surfaces. Sprinkle with sugar, coating completely. Shake off excess sugar, and lay on waxed paper until dry. Store in an airtight container. Keeps indefinitely.

Easy-to-Grow Recipe Substitutes

Lemony French sorrel. Out of lemons? Pluck a few leaves of French sorrel *(Rumex scutatus)*. Finely minced, the sour leaves give tuna, pasta, and chicken salads a lemony twist.

Easy nasturtium capers. Pickled nasturtium flower buds *(Tropaeolum majus)* and unripe seedpods make great capers. Harvest buds while they're still tight, and seedpods before they harden. Place them in a clean glass bottle and cover with vinegar. They'll be ready to eat in three days and will keep well for at least a year. No need to refrigerate.

Lovely lovage. Lovage *(Levisticum officinale)* is a beautiful perennial herb with a distinct celery flavor — and much easier to grow than celery. Start from seed or buy transplants. Place in sun or part shade in moisture-retentive soil. One or two plants will produce a continuous supply of leaves and stalks to mince for salads and stews. A little lovage goes a long way — use it in the same proportion as most other culinary herbs for seasoning.

Sunny calendula. Although they have little flavor, calendula petals *(Calendula officinalis)* are an inexpensive substitute when you want a saffron color.

Spicy nigella seeds. The seeds of *Nigella sativa*, sometimes called black cumin or black caraway, have a slightly peppery, nutty taste and can be used in place of black pepper. They have been used since biblical times to flavor breads, stews, salads, and condiments. In fact, nigella seeds, not poppy seeds, dotted the first New York bagels. This easy-to-grow annual produces decorative parchment-colored seedpods, which dry naturally and self-sow readily once established. You may have to buy these seeds from a spice purveyor, since not many gardening suppliers carry them. Seeds of the more common *Nigella damascena*, commonly known as love-in-a-mist, have little flavor.

CHAPTER 7

COOKING

Herbs A to Z

ou can grow a great many herbs to enjoy in your everyday cooking. But because this book, like your garden, has a limited amount of space, I selected the most popular cooking herbs, those that are easiest to grow and offer the most versatility. In this chapter you'll find growing and cooking tips for herbs you already enjoy, and also ideas for new herbs, including the best culinary cultivars, to add to your garden. You'll find details about growing each herb, such as what type of soil, light, and moisture conditions are needed, as well as the many ways you can use these herbs in the kitchen. You'll also discover tips for harvesting, drying, and storage, and quite simply how to enjoy your garden and the harvest, whether you have a large herb garden, a few herbs tucked into flower or vegetable beds, or pots of herbs growing on your deck or balcony.

BASIL *Ocimum basilicum*
Plant type: Annual

When the first printed cookbook appeared in
1475, readers were advised that basil produced
madness; in addition, when it was pounded and
covered with stone, scorpions would arise!
Over time, however, basil has become one of
the most popular cooking herbs in many
countries, and is especially associated with
Italian cooking. Italian girls wear a sprig of basil
behind an ear to invite a kiss.

Basil

Uses. Sweet basil is the most popular pesto herb and is excellent for
seasoning summer vegetables like tomatoes. Lemon basil pairs with
fish (try a cultivar called 'Mrs. Burns', which bolts less readily than
other types); cinnamon basil is good with fruits and spicy dishes;
holy basil is exotic in fruits and beverages; and opal basil is a beautiful
accent plant with leaves that produce a stunning herb vinegar. Basil
flowers are good edible garnishes. Try using the spicy seeds like
poppy seeds.

In the garden. Sturdy branching plants range in height from
6 inches to 3 feet. Sow seed indoors 4 to 6 weeks before the last frost
date, covering seed lightly, or outdoors after the soil has warmed.
Most varieties need temperatures around 70°F. Seed will germinate
in 7 days. Transplant to a sunny spot in the garden when the soil is
warm. Allow 6 to 8 inches betweeen mini-leaved varieties; 12 to 18
inches between larger plants. This annual also makes a good container plant. In the vegetable garden, basil is said to benefit both
asparagus and tomatoes by keeping pests away.

Harvesting and preserving. Snip fresh sprigs as needed. Flavor is
best just as buds begin to appear. Most basils perish at the very mention of frost, so harvest all your basil before the threat of the first
frost. Holy basil is somewhat hardier than other basils, and it's also
the only basil with seed hardy enough to self-sow. Basil is best preserved by freezing, as a paste or in pesto.

BAY *Laurus nobilis*

Also known as: Sweet bay, laurel
Plant type: Tender perennial

Bay has long been a symbol of victory and excellence, dating back to when ancient Greek and Roman kings, poets, scholars, and athletes were crowned with wreaths made of bay leaves. The leaves have a lemon flavor.

Uses. An essential componet in *bouquet garni,* the pungent leaves are also used to flavor hearty soups and stews. Try adding a leaf to the pot in which you're cooking pasta. Place dried leaves in cupboards and in containers of stored grains to discourage weevils.

In the garden. This evergreen shrub grows to 40 feet in its native habitat, but you can grow it as a container plant where it will grow to only about 6 feet. Pot in rich, well-drained potting soil with a pH of 6.0 to 7.0. In areas with hot summers, bay prefers partial shade. Although bay tolerates light frosts, bring it indoors before temperatures fall to 28°F. Indoors, grow bay in bright light and cool (55 to 65°F) temperatures. It's subject to scale; swab leaf surfaces with rubbing alcohol if you detect any problem. *Zones 8-9.*

Harvesting and preserving. Snip fresh leaves as needed. Bay leaves dry easily if you choose not to overwinter a plant. Separate leaves from stems and lay on racks.

Bay

BEE BALM *Monarda* species

Also known as: Bergamot, Oswego tea
Plant type: Perennial

The name "bee balm" refers to the plant's ability to relieve the pain of bee stings. The next time you get stung in the garden, crush or chew a bee balm leaf and rub it on the spot. It's also soothing on minor burns. The dryland species, *Monarda fistulosa,* figures prominently in Native American herbals.

Bee balm

Bee balm, particularly plants with red flowers, is very attractive to hummingbirds. Although bee balm is unrelated to the tropical shrub called bergamot, its pungent, minty taste reminded colonists of bergamot-flavored Earl Grey tea. Some cooks use it as a substitute for epazoté in Mexican cooking. The flowers are sweetly spicy.

Uses. Use bee balm leaves and flowers in tea, for a sweet but spicy mint-flavored drink. The blossoms also make a beautiful, edible garnish.

In the garden. Clump-forming, upright plants grow 2 to 4 feet tall, with disks of tubular flowers appearing in early summer. Red, pink, white, and lavender cultivars are available. Purchase a transplant or dig divisions from a friend's garden. Allow 18 to 24 inches between plants. Bee balm enjoys moist soil and partial shade, but it can be invasive. Cut back to 6 inches after blooming to encourage a second flush and to help control powdery mildew. *Zones 4–9.*

Harvesting and preserving. Clip fresh sprigs or single leaves as needed. Bee balm dries easily and retains good flavor. Hang-dry stalks before blooming, when mildewed leaves are less likely and leaf flavor is best. Use flowers fresh for garnishes. Dry flowers on racks to use in baked goods like scones.

BORAGE *Borago officinalis*
Also known as: Talewort
Plant type: Hardy annual

Long associated with the heart, borage is thought to boost courage. In the late 1500s, the herbalist Gerard wrote, "A sirup concocted of the floures quietith the lunatick person and leaves eaten raw do engender good blood."

Uses. The fuzzy leaves have a pronounced cucumber flavor useful in beverages, traditionally wine and Pimm's cup (a gin-based aperitif), but also nice in wine spritzers, lemonade, fruit drinks, punches, salads, and herb vinegars. Mince fine if eating raw. The flowers, fresh or candied, make a beautiful garnish.

Borage

In the garden. Borage has hairy gray-green leaves on floppy plants, 18 to 24 inches tall. Glistening, star-shaped, sky blue flowers appear throughout the summer. (There is also a white-flowered variety.) Start seed directly in the garden or in pots, as transplanting is tricky. Seed germinates quickly at 60 to 70°F; cover seed to twice its thickness. Allow 18 to 24 inches between plants. Once established, borage will self-sow reliably for years. Grow it in sun or partial shade. It grows best during the cooler ends of the gardening season.

Harvesting and preserving. Clip fresh sprigs or single leaves as needed. Preserve leaves by freezing. The flowers can be candied for edible garnishes (see page 121) or dried in silica gel for crafts.

BURNET *Poterium sanguisorba*
Also known as: Salad burnet
Plant type: Perennial

Burnet gets its botanic name *Poterium*, which means "drinking cup," from its use in cool, refreshing beverages.

Burnet

Uses. Burnet's cucumber-flavored leaves are nice in salads, herb butters, and vinegars, as well as cold drinks and herb teas. Both leaves and flowers make a lovely garnish.

In the garden. A short-lived perennial, burnet grows in a mound, with fernlike leaves on 10-inch-tall stems, and produces reddish pink, berrylike flowers in May. It can be evergreen in milder areas. Start it from seed in late autumn or in early spring where it is to grow. Thin to 12 inches between plants. Indoors, it needs light and 70°F temperatures to germinate. Transplant while seedlings are small. Keep buds pinched to boost leaf production. Unless burnet self-sows in your garden, it's easiest to purchase one or two new transplants each year. Burnet grows best in well-drained, alkaline soils. *Zones 4–7.*

Harvesting and preserving. Clip fresh leaf stalks at soil level. To preserve, freeze leaves or add them to vinegar. Flowers hang-dry well, if desired; cut stems just before buds open.

CALENDULA *Calendula officinalis*

Also known as: Pot marigold
Plant type: Hardy annual

Although no relation to African or French marigolds, calendula is called pot marigold in the old herbals because it was grown in cool greenhouses for winter bloom. Its Latin name refers to its ability to bloom every month of the year in some climates.

Calendula

Uses. Use calendula petals to add saffron color (though little flavor) to rice and soups, or strew them over casseroles as a colorful garnish. Float a calendula flower in a cup of tea for good cheer!

In the garden. Calendula is a branching plant, 8 to 24 inches tall, with smooth, oblong leaves and daisylike yellow, gold, orange, and apricot flowers. Start from seed indoors (soil temperature 55 to 68°F), or sow outdoors in mid-spring and again in late summer. Thin to 12 to 18 inches. Calendula self-sows faithfully once established. It prefers full sun but will accept partial shade, especially in hot areas. It blooms from late spring until hard frost, although it slows down during the hottest part of summer, then comes back in cool weather if you deadhead to encourage flowering.

Harvesting and preserving. Clip fresh flowers soon after they open fully. Dry flowerheads whole on racks (finish off in a low-heat oven before storing), or pull off petals and dry on paper towels.

CHERVIL *Anthriscus cerefolium*

Also known as: Salad chervil
Plant type: Hardy annual

Twenty centuries ago, chervil was well known to the Greeks and Romans who used it medicinally. In cooking, it is often substituted for tarragon, which cannot be grown from seed.

Uses. Chervil is one of the essential ingredients in *fines herbes*. The leaves have a delicate anise (licorice)

Chervil

flavor, considered indispensable in French cooking. Chervil is much underused in American cookery, probably because it loses flavor when dried and it's difficult to buy fresh in markets.

In the garden. A hardy annual, similar in appearance to parsley, chervil has finely dissected, lacy leaves and tiny white flowers. If possible, buy one or two transplants in early spring. Chervil grows quickly, blooms, and goes to seed in early summer. Collect some of the seeds (seeds must be fresh to germinate, so it can be difficult to purchase viable seed), and sow them in late summer where plants are to grow. Thin seedlings to 9 to 12 inches apart. Chervil also self-sows readily in moist, rich soil in partial shade. A good spot is around the compost pile or behind a garden gate. You should get a fall crop sown from plants that bloomed in spring.

Harvesting and preserving. Clip stems at the soil level before flowers are fully developed. To preserve, freeze leaves or make herb butter.

CHIVES *Allium schoenoprasum*
Also known as: Onion chives
Plant type: Perennial

Add the tender shoots of this early spring plant to your salad, and you'll know that the garden season has begun. Onion chives are daintier than garlic chives (see page 130). They may go dormant and disappear altogether by the end of a hot summer.

Chives

Uses. Both the tubular blades and pink blossoms have a mild onion flavor. The leaves are used to garnish or to flavor dips, spreads, and delicate dishes like omelets. The flowers make a beautiful rose-tinted herb vinegar.

In the garden. Chives grow in clumps of hollow, round-bladed leaves. Pink powderpuff flowers blossom in early spring. Buy two or three transplants or separate a friend's clump. Space clumps 8 to 12 inches apart. Chives will self-sow modestly if seed heads are not removed. Chives grow best in full sun in well-drained soil. *Zones 3–9.*

Harvesting and preserving. To harvest, cut individual blades at ground level from the outside of the plant. Don't shear, as this may destroy the flowering stalks. Preserve leaves by freezing. To dry flower-heads, cut flower stalks at the base just after the flower "cap" drops off and hang-dry; or remove the blossoms and dry on racks.

Garlic chives

CHIVES, GARLIC *Allium tuberosum*
Also known as: Chinese chives or Chinese leeks
Plant type: Perennial

Unlike onion chives (see page 129), garlic chives have flat rather than tubular leaf blades, and they bloom in the fall, a welcome trait, as many other perennial herbs are spring and early summer bloomers. The white blossoms are sweet-scented and attractive to bees, and the flowerheads dry well for ornamental uses.

Uses. The greens of garlic chives are very nutritious and have a mild garlic flavor most people tolerate easily. Use leaf blades and unopened flower stalks generously in stir-fries and salads. The flowers are also edible and good in herbal vinegars.

In the garden. Garlic chives grow best in the cooler ends of the season. Buy two or three transplants or separate a clump from a friend's garden. Space them 12 to 18 inches apart. The clumps spread much more quickly than onion chives. Garlic chives prefer full sun, but also grow well in partial shade. They can be potted and grown indoors in a sunny window for a modest supply of fresh greens during the winter. Plants self-sow overabundantly if seed heads are allowed to shatter. For easiest care, and to encourage better leaf production, allow only a few plants to bloom. *Zones 3–9.*

Harvesting and preserving. Clip greens at the soil level from the outside of the clump. Preserve leaves by freezing. To dry flowerheads, cut flower stalks at the base just after the flower "cap" drops off and hang-dry, or remove the blossoms and dry them on racks.

CORIANDER *Coriandrum sativum*

Also known as: Cilantro, Chinese parsley

Plant type: Hardy annual

One of the traditional bitter Passover herbs, coriander has been cultivated since biblical times. The common name stems from the Greek *koros* ("bug"), perhaps because some people find the odor of the leaves offensive. The ripe seeds have a warm, spicy flavor.

Uses. The seeds, which are generally called coriander, are a favorite spice in the foods of many European countries and India. Southeast Asian and Mexican cuisines often feature the greens, known by the Spanish name *cilantro*. In the United States, the greens are especially popular in salsa and Thai dishes.

In the garden. Coriander has white flowers and flat, parsley-like leaves on floppy stems that reach 2 feet in height. In early spring or late summer, sow this hardy annual where you want it to grow. Allow 4 to 6 inches between plants. Coriander bolts in hot weather. It self-sows once established; the seeds are large and stay on the plant for quite some time, so they're easy to collect, either for cooking or to sow the following year. If you're growing coriander for the leaves, select varieties such as 'Santo' or 'Slo-bolt', which tolerate hot weather a little better than other varieties.

Harvesting and preserving. Cut fresh sprigs or remove entire stalks as needed. Preserve leaves by freezing. The seeds are easy to gather; store them in airtight containers.

Coriander

DILL *Anethum graveolens*

Plant type: Hardy annual

Dill is a short-lived, tall, graceful, and somewhat showy herb that makes a good background plant for other herbs. It aids plants in the cabbage family by repelling the moth that lays cabbageworm eggs. Some beneficial insects,

Dill

like honeybees and tiny parasitic wasps, love it. It's also a host for swallowtail butterfly caterpillars. The word "dill" is derived from an Anglo-Saxon word meaning "to lull," referring to its soothing properties. Dill water (also known as gripe water) is still given to babies in Britain to relieve colic and help induce sleep.

Uses. Dill leaves, often called dillweed, have a mildly piquant flavor, traditionally coupled with poached and smoked fish as well as eggs and salads. Dill seed is a spicy seasoning used for pickles, salads, and sauces, and can be used like caraway seed to flavor pumpernickel and rye breads.

In the garden. Dill has lime green, very fine fernlike foliage on graceful hollow stems, which reach to 18 to 48 inches tall. It bears flat clusters of tiny yellow flowers. Dill prefers cool, moist soil. In early spring, sow seed on the surface of the soil where you want it to grow. Thin seedlings to allow 6 to 8 inches between plants. For a ready supply of leaves and flower heads, succession plant every 3 to 4 weeks until midsummer; sow again in late summer. Dill self-sows once established.

Harvesting and preserving. Cut sprigs or entire stalks as needed. Dillweed is best fresh, but it can be frozen, or dried in the refrigerator (see page 114). Harvest the seeds when they turn brown. If they're still a little soft when harvested, leave them on a screen to dry. (To test for dryness, check to be sure that they break, rather than bend.)

FENNEL *Foeniculum vulgare*
Plant type: Perennial

During the Middle Ages, fennel was considered one of the "nine sacred herbs," and a sprig hung in the home was believed to ward off the evil eye. Fennel is closely related to dill, coriander, chervil, and carrots. Its seed is a well-known antidote for gas, indigestion, and colic. Fennel is a good nectar source for bees and beneficial wasps, and a host for the swallowtail butterfly caterpillar.

Fennel

Uses. Fennel is grown for its seeds and fernlike leaves, both of which have a sweet anise flavor. The leaves are a superb seasoning for fish and eggs. The seeds are used in pastries and pickles and also to flavor the liqueur anisette. Florence fennel *(F. vulgare* var. *azoricum)* is cultivated as a vegetable for its thick, anise-flavored stalks and bulb.

In the garden. Similar in appearance to dill, fennel bears umbels of small yellow flowers on ribbed stems that can reach 3 to 5 feet in height; a giant form can easily reach 8 feet. Sow seed in the garden on the surface of the soil as early in spring as possible. It self-sows once established. A bronze-colored form (available as several cultivars, including 'Rubrum', 'Purpurascens', and 'Bronze') features striking coppery foliage that is especially beautiful in autumn. The foliage of bronze fennel is sweeter than green fennel's, with a spicy overtone. Try it in crab or egg salad. *Zones 6–9.*

Harvesting and preserving. Cut fresh sprigs or stalks as needed. Fennel leaves are best fresh but they can be frozen. Harvest seed heads when dry but before they shatter.

Scented geranium

GERANIUM, SCENTED *Pelargonium* species
Plant type: Tender perennial, grown as an annual

Of the many "flavors" of scented geranium, the rose-scented leaves have the most culinary value, but all the varieties make fragrant and beautiful foliage plants.

Uses. Steep the leaves to flavor the liquid that will be used in baking. They are also good in sauces and to flavor herb honey. The flowers are edible, but not showy.

In the garden. Woody branching plants grow 18 to 36 inches tall, depending on the variety. Buy transplants or take cuttings from a mature plant, and grow as a container plant in sun or in partial shade. Trim regularly to maintain a neat habit. For indoor growing, cool temperatures (55 to 65°F) and bright light are ideal. *Zone 10.*

Harvesting and preserving. Clip leaves or tender sprigs for fresh use. Rose-scented geranium leaves dry well and retain both good flavor and fragrance. Remove the stems from the leaves and dry them on racks or screens.

LAVENDER *Lavandula* species
Plant type: Perennial

Lavender is derived from the Latin *lavare* meaning "to wash." In seventeenth century Europe, lavender was a common household item, used to perfume the wash, to protect clothing from moths, and to mask the overripe odors of daily living. It is still very popular for its fragrance, and although it's less well known as a culinary herb, it adds an unusual sweet spiciness to teas and desserts.

Lavender

Uses. Lavender buds are used to flavor tea and pastries. Lavender is also grown as a drought-resistant and deer-proof ornamental, and is much beloved by bees.

In the garden. English lavenders are small (18 to 24 inches), shrubby perennial plants with narrow gray leaves and spikes of tiny fragrant flowers in blue, lavender, purple, white, and pink. Buy transplants or take cuttings from a friend's garden. Plant in early spring in alkaline, well-drained soil. (Lavender will not tolerate poorly drained soil.) If you trim plants after the spring flowering, they may bloom again in early autumn. To maintain vigor and appearance, prune in late winter and then again in early spring to remove any dead wood. In areas with unreliable snow cover, mulch with evergreen branches after Christmas.

In addition to English lavenders, look for the French hybrid lavandins (a cross between *L. angustifolia* and *L. latifolia*), which are becoming more commonly available. Lavandins are larger, up to 4 feet, and less subject to winterkill. They produce stunning 2-foot flower stems in blue and purple hues. You won't likely see the word "lavandin" when buying plants — look for cultivar names like

'Provence', 'Grosso', 'Dutch', and 'Seal'. Many varieties of lavender are not frost hardy, so unless you live in Zones 7–10, do not buy fringed lavender (*L. dentata*) or French lavender (*L. stoechas*) for outdoor gardens. *Zones 5–10.*

Harvesting and preserving. Harvest flower stalks just when the buds begin to show color, and hang-dry.

LEMONGRASS *Cymbopogon citratus*

Also known as: West Indian lemon, fevergrass
Plant type: Tender perennial

The sweet fragrance and mild lemony flavor is indispensable in Southeast Asian dishes.
Uses. The fleshy base of the leaf stalks are chopped and cooked in sauces and soups and also pounded with other spices to make a marinade.

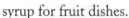

Lemongrass

Lemongrass stalks also make a subtly flavored tea or syrup for fruit dishes.

In the garden. This clump-forming tropical grass grows 2 to 3 feet tall with wide green blades. Buy a transplant and place it in a pot of rich soil in full sun. Keep it well watered, and by summer's end your clump will be 3 feet wide. Although lemongrass isn't the easiest plant to grow indoors, you might like to try to prepare a plant or two for next season. Cut back the plant to 2 or 3 inches tall, pull apart the roots, and plant several pots, one transplant to each pot. Place pots in your warmest, sunniest window, and fertilize once a month. *Zone 10.*

Harvesting and preserving. Choose outside stems about ½-inch thick. (By the way, proceed carefully, as those grassy blades have sharp edges.) With sharp scissors or a knife, cut each stem at the base. Cut off and discard the leafy upper section. You can then cut the stems into 2- to 3-inch lengths and slice them in half to better release the flavor. Unless pounded, the stalks remain tough and are generally strained out before eating. Harvest the entire plant before frost. Freeze stalks in self-sealing plastic bags.

LEMON VERBENA *Aloysia triphylla*

Plant type: Tender perennial

Lemon verbena was known to the Incas, but it did
not reach North America until the eighteenth century.
In Mexico it's often called *yerba Louisa*.

Uses. The leaves make a wonderful addition to tea and
are also used to flavor syrups. Strain the leaves before
serving, as they remain tough even afer cooking.

In the garden. Because it's a tropical shrub, lemon
verbena is best treated as a large container plant in
temperate climates. Buy a transplant or take cuttings in early spring.
Pot it in good potting soil and transplant into larger pots as it grows.
Place it in full sun and water every day or two in warm weather unless
rains provide. To overwinter, cut the plant back to about 15 inches in
the fall. Because it's deciduous, it will probably drop its leaves when
you bring it indoors. Keep it in a sunny window or under a grow light
where temperatures remain above 60°F, water it enough to keep the
soil moist, and within about 10 days it will sprout new leaves.

Harvesting and preserving. Clip leaves or short sprigs for fresh use.
The leaves dry practically overnight and retain excellent flavor. Separate
them from the stems, and lay them on paper towels or racks to dry.

Lemon
verbena

LOVAGE *Levisticum officinale*

Plant type: Perennial

Important as a medicinal plant in earlier times,
lovage is now primarily a potherb valued for
its intense celery flavor. The hollow stalks
make tasty straws for vegetable drinks like
tomato juice.

Use. Add lovage stalks and leaves to soups
and stews, as well as herb vinegars and butters.
Use it sparingly, as the flavor is quite pronounced.

Lovage

In the garden. Lovage has hollow, celery-like stems. It can grow up to 6 feet tall with flat clusters of yellow flowers in midsummer. Place one or two plants in moist, rich soil in full sun to partial shade, allowing 2 to 3 feet per plant. Divide mature plants in early spring. *Zones 5–8.*
Harvesting and preserving. Cut fresh stalks at ground level or clip leafy sprigs. Use lovage fresh, as it doesn't dry well. You can puree and freeze small quantities for use in soups and stews (see page 116).

MARJORAM, SWEET *Origanum majorana*

Also known as: Knotted marjoram
Plant type: Tender perennial

Sweet marjoram

Pot marjoram *(O. onites),* also known as Greek oregano, and wild marjoram *(O. vulgare)* are hardy perennials, but their flavor doesn't compare to the more tender *O. majorana.* The Greeks named marjoram "joy of the mountains" and used it to crown newlyweds, believing it to symbolize marital bliss.
Uses. Marjoram is one of the most versatile and universally appealing flavorings. The taste is warm, with a touch of lemon and mint. Use with chicken, fish, eggs, and vegetables. Try it instead of oregano in tomato sauces and as a substitute for sage in sausage. It's also good in herb butters and teas.
In the garden. Sweet marjoram has velvety oval leaves on sprawling plants. Buy transplants in mid-spring, and grow them in full sun or light shade, in the ground or in a container. Allow 8 to 12 inches between plants. Keep buds clipped to encourage leaf production. The plants grow best in the cooler ends of the season. When temperatures threaten to dip below 28°F, bring plants indoors. Sweet marjoram makes a good houseplant if you give it bright light and cool temperatures. *Zones 9–10.*
Harvesting and preserving. Clip fresh sprigs as needed. Marjoram retains good flavor when dried. Hang-dry stalks just before buds appear, and finish off in a low-heat oven before storing.

MEXICAN MARIGOLD *Tagetes lucida*

Also known as: Texas marigold mint, Mexican mint

Plant type: Tender perennial

The leaves of Mexican marigold taste remarkably like tarragon. However, it is generally easier to grow and more abundant than tarragon, especially in hot, humid climates.

Mexican marigold

Uses. The leaves, fresh or dried, are used in any way that you might use tarragon. Use it more sparingly, though, as the flavor is stronger. Mexican marigold is a staple in Southwestern dishes featuring corn, chayote, and fowl. Try it also in herb tea. The small flowers have a mild flavor and are attractive in goat cheese spreads and herb butter.

In the garden. This lanky marigold has skinny leaves and small golden flowers that appear in late summer. It reaches a height of 1½ feet. It's easy to start from seed; sow indoors 6 weeks before the last frost date in warm (70 to 75°F) soil, barely covering seeds. It germinates in 5 to 7 days. Set plants in full sun after the soil is warm. Allow 6 to 9 inches between plants. In colder areas, treat it as an annual. If your growing season is long enough, save seeds to plant next season. *Zones 9–10.*

Harvesting and preserving. Clip fresh sprigs as needed. Mexican marigold dries easily and retains good flavor. Hang-dry stalks before blooms appear. Dry blossoms on racks or screens.

MINT *Mentha* species

Plant type: Perennial

According to the sixteenth century herbalist Gerard, "The smell rejoiceth the heart of man." Mint is a well-known remedy for digestive upsets and bad breath. For culinary purposes, choose peppermint, spearmint, 'Chocolate' mint *(M. piperita)*, and 'Blue Balsam' mint *(M. piperita)*.

Peppermint

Uses. I like 'Blue Balsam' mint dry or fresh for tea and to flavor sauces and syrups for fruits and other sweets. Spearmint is especially delicious with peas; mint also flavors the traditional jelly served with lamb.

In the garden. Bushy and sprawling, mints grow 18 to 36 inches tall, with square stems, pointed green leaves, and spikes of small purple, pink, and white flowers. Buy a transplant, take a cutting, or dig a division from an established clump. Allow 18 to 24 inches between plants. Mints adapt to full sun or dense shade and a wide variety of soil conditions, but they grow best in moist soil in partial shade. They spread quickly and can become invasive. Plant mints where you can cut them back with the lawn mower, or plant them in sunken containers to minimize their invasiveness. Plant each kind of mint in a separate location or bees will cross-pollinate them and their distinct flavors will be lost. To renew worn-out mint plantings, dig out old clumps, discard woody roots, and add compost to stimulate new growth. Mints are often infected by a mite that leaves red spots on the leaves, but this doesn't affect the vitality or flavor. *Zones 5–9.*

Harvesting and preserving. Clip fresh sprigs as needed. Mint dries easily and retains good flavor. Hang-dry stalks before blossoms appear.

NASTURTIUM *Tropaeolum majus*
Plant type: Annual

In Latin, nasturtium means "nose twist," from the peppery smell of its leaves. The leaves and flowers have been used in European salads since their discovery by explorers in the mountains of Peru in the late sixteenth century. Nasturtium leaves contain 10 times more vitamin C than lettuce!

Uses. Part of the watercress family, nasturtium leaves and flowers have a sharp, peppery flavor. Mince the leaves finely and use in soft cheese spreads and salads. The flowers are beautiful edible garnishes and can be stuffed with fillings like guacamole. Pickle the seeds while they're still soft to make a good substitute for capers.

Nasturtium

In the garden. There are two types of these annual plants: a bushy type that grows 8 to 18 inches tall, and a vine that sprawls up to 6 feet. The latter is pictured in photographs of Monet's garden. Both have round leaves like lily pads on long stems, and large tubular flowers in bright shades of yellow, orange, and red. Start seeds indoors 2 to 3 weeks before the last frost, or plant them in the garden bed after the soil is warm and danger of frost has passed. Plant the large seeds ½ inch deep and 6 to 9 inches apart. Keep the soil moist until seeds germinate, usually within 7 to 10 days. Place in full sun to light shade. Nasturtiums make good container and trellis plants. Black plant lice are attracted to nasturtiums in the cooler ends of the season. Dislodge them with a sharp spray of cold water, or use insecticidal soap to control them. To discourage the ants that bring aphids to the plants, pour vegetable oil over their nests.

Harvesting and preserving. Flowers and leaves should be used fresh. Stems will last in a vase of water for several days. Seeds may be pickled.

OREGANO *Origanum vulgare*

Also known as: Wild marjoram, pot marjoram
Plant type: Perennial

Oregano wasn't well known in the United States until after World War II, when the pizza craze followed the troops home. Up until this time, American cooks used few herbs in their cooking, but during their stay in Europe, GIs tasted and enjoyed many different herbs, especially some of the favorite Mediterranean herbs like oregano and basil. Food in the United States would never be the same again.

Oregano

Uses. Popular in many Greek and Italian dishes, oregano leaves are the most common seasoning for tomato and pizza sauce. Oregano is used to flavor a wide variety of foods, including poultry, fish, vegetables, cheese, and sausage.

In the garden. These bushy perennials grow 1 to 2 feet tall, with small rounded leaves and clusters of tiny white or pink flowers that bloom in late summer. When you buy a transplant, smell and taste the leaves, if possible, as it can be difficult to find plants with good oregano flavor. Plant in full sun, allowing 9 to 12 inches between plants. Clip flower buds to stimulate fresh leaf production. *O. heracleoticum* is considered by many to be the true oregano. I routinely substitute sweet marjoram for oregano. *Zones 5–9.*

Harvesting and preserving. Clip fresh sprigs as needed. Oregano dries easily and retains good flavor. Hang-dry stalks before blossoming.

PAPALO *Porophyllum ruderale* spp. *macrocephalum*

Also known as: Mexican coriander
Plant type: Annual

Papalo is a popular seasoning in Mexico and the Southwestern United States, where it grows wild. Some restaurants feature a branch of the herb in a glass of water on the table, encouraging diners to pinch a leaf and roll it up in tortillas.

Papalo

Uses. Leaves make an abundant hot-weather substitute for cilantro; its flavor is similar to that of cilantro, but more pungent. Use fresh as a garnish for salsa, tacos, gazpacho, and other Southwestern dishes.

In the garden. Papalo is a naturally bushy annual with rounded, misty green leaves. It's large, reaching up to 6 to 8 feet in one season, but it's easy to grow from seed. Start several seeds indoors two or three weeks before the last frost, and transplant outdoors once the soil is warm. Allow 3 feet between plants. (One plant is plenty for most families!) A related species is quillquina *(P. ruderale),* or "killi," a shorter plant (4 to 5 feet) from Bolivia. It's somewhat sweeter than papalo.

Harvesting and preserving. Leaves are best fresh. Clip sprigs as needed. Collect seed for the next season if your growing season is long enough to produce seed.

PARSLEY *Petroselinum crispum*

Plant type: Biennial

Parsley is very nutritious, especially high in iron and vitamins A, B, and C. It's also a well-known breath freshener.

Uses. Parsley enhances the flavor of most foods and is a familiar ingredient in soups, stews, salads, pasta sauces, herb blends, and herb butters. Parsley also makes good pesto, singly or combined with other herbs. For best flavor, use Italian, or flat-leafed, parsley *(P. crispum* 'Neapolitanum'); use curly varieties as a garnish.

In the garden. This familiar biennial herb is usually grown as an annual for culinary purposes. Buy two or three transplants in early spring, and plant them in rich, moist soil in full sun to partial shade. Allow 8–12 inches between plants. Parsley will often overwinter, and you can use the first flush of leaf growth in the spring, but the leaves will soon become limp and lose their flavor as the plant goes to seed.

Harvesting and preserving. Clip stalks at soil level as needed. Parsley is best fresh, although it dries well in the refrigerator (see page 114), which is helpful if you want to mix it into dry herb blends. You can also freeze it, especially as a paste or in pesto.

ROSEMARY *Rosmarinus officinalis*

Plant type: Tender perennial

Legend holds that the blue of the blossoms derives from the Virgin Mary's cloak, which brushed against the plant during the flight to Egypt. The expression "rosemary for remembrance" relates to its reputation for strengthening the memory: Students in ancient Greece were said to wear rosemary wreaths while studying. Recent research seems to bear this out, as James Duke reports in his book *The Green Pharmacy* that the antioxidants in rosmarinic acid may help prevent memory loss associated with aging.

Uses. Rosemary is a strongly flavored herb, generally used alone rather than in combination with other herbs. The piney flavor of the leaves complement chicken, fish, lamb, pork, and cheese dishes, as well as breads like focaccia. Perk up a cup of Earl Grey tea by adding a sprig of rosemary. The flowers make dainty edible garnishes.

In the garden. Rosemary is a woody shrub growing to 3 feet or more, with resinous pine needlelike leaves and small flowers in blue, pink, or white. Buy transplants or root cuttings from a mature plant. In areas with cold winters rosemary is best treated as a container plant. Place it in full sun. Keep rosemary on the dry side, but don't forget about it, as it won't recover if it dries out completely. A prostrate form with weeping branches *(R. officinalis* 'Prostatus') makes an excellent container plant as well. Some cultivars, such as 'Arp', are touted to survive Zone 6–7 winters if grown in a sheltered spot. *Zones 8-10.*

Harvesting and preserving. Clip fresh sprigs as needed. Rosemary dries easily and retains its flavor. Hang-dry stalks before flowers appear.

SAGE *Salvia officinalis*
Plant type: Perennial

The word "salvia" comes from the Latin *salvere,* meaning "to be saved," and refers to sage's many healing uses. "Why should a man die whilst sage grows in his garden?" is an old Roman proverb. In addition to *S. officinalis,* other sage species can be used for culinary purposes, too. Cleveland sage *(S. clevelandii),* a tender perennial (Zones 8–10), has an intoxicating resinous perfume; use it sparingly (one or two leaves) to flavor poultry stuffing, or to flavor cheese spreads and herb butters. Another is pineapple sage *(S. elegans),* a tender perennial (Zones 8–10) with showy red blossoms that appear in late summer. Its fresh leaves make a nice tea (they lose their flavor when dried), and the flowers are a beautiful sweet garnish. There are hundreds of strictly ornamental varieties of *Salvia* as well.

Sage

Uses. Sage leaves are the traditional seasoning for Thanksgiving turkey stuffing and are also used to flavor game, sausage, onions, beans, eggplant, tomatoes, peas, and cheese. Fresh sage has a more delicate flavor than dried sage.

In the garden. Sage is a woody shrub with gray-green, rough-textured leaves; it grows 12 to 30 inches tall. Buy one or two transplants, or take cuttings from a mature plant. Plant in full sun to light shade in average soil, allowing 2 feet per plant. Most varieties will bloom in early summer — let the bees have a treat! Remove spent flower stalks after blooming, and cut the plant back by about a third to encourage fresh leaf growth. Prune again in the fall or early spring to maintain a neat shape. Plants tend to become woody after a few years. Take cuttings or layerings to establish new plantings. Some good culinary cultivars are 'Berggarten', which has a few very small-blue flowers but large, silver-gray oval leaves that are covered with a fine, whitish fuzz; 'Holt's Mammoth', a vigorous green-leaved cultivar; and 'Woodcote', which has very large leaves and tiny white flowers, and which resists powdery mildew. *Zones 4–8.*

Harvesting and preserving. Clip fresh sprigs as needed. Sage leaves are thick and resinous, and thus dry slowly. Hang-dry stalks and finish off the drying process in a low-heat oven before storing.

SUMMER SAVORY *Satureja hortensis*

Plant type: Annual

Savory's Latin name derives from the Roman word for "satyr," a mythical creature given to lascivious behavior. This herb was considered to be an aphrodisiac, hence the association. In Germany, savory is called *Bohenkraut,* the green bean herb. Savory is thought to improve digestion. There is a perennial type called winter savory *(S. montana),* but the flavor is too sharp for my taste. It is sometimes used for herbal hedges.

Summer savory

Uses. Savory is an excellent seasoning for vegetables, especially beans and squash, as well as poultry and fish dishes. Cooks who don't care for sage often rely on savory instead. The peppery flavor also makes a nice substitute for black pepper. Use it to flavor teas, herb butters, and flavored vinegars. Winter savory may be used for meats and patés.

In the garden. A sprawling annual plant 12 to 18 inches tall, savory has small gray-green leaves and tiny pinkish flowers. Buy two or three transplants, or start seeds indoors 2 or 3 weeks before the last frost or outdoors after the soil warms. For germination, it needs a temperature of 70°F; barely cover the seed. Set plants in full sun, allowing 6 inches for each plant. Mound soil around plants if they begin to flop. If plants run to seed, sow again in midsummer. Savory often self-sows, reappearing the following season when the soil warms.

Harvesting and preserving. Clip fresh sprigs as needed. Savory dries easily and retains good flavor. Hang-dry stalks just before buds appear.

TARRAGON, FRENCH
Artemisia dracunculus var. *sativa*
Also known as: Estragon
Plant type: Perennial

Tarragon leaves have a peculiar numbing effect on the tongue, hence the common name from the French *estragon*, which means "little dragon." Ancient physicians advised patients to nibble some French tarragon to numb the taste buds before taking a bitter potion.

Tarragon

Uses. Tarragon has a unique anise-like flavor, which is practically synonymous with French cuisine. The leaves are used to flavor fish, chicken, poultry, eggs, and cheese. Tarragon is also a very popular herbal vinegar.

In the garden. Tarragon is a perennial plant with 2-foot-long, branched stems and narrow leaves. Buy one or two transplants of French tarragon, as it does not set viable seed. Propagate by root divisions. Plant in full sun in well-drained soil, allowing 12 to 18 inches per plant. Avoid purchasing Russian tarragon *(A. dracunculoides)* for culinary use, as it is a different species with little flavor. *Zones 4–8.*

Harvesting: Clip fresh sprigs as needed. It's excellent for flavoring vinegar. Tarragon dries easily and retains good flavor. Hang-dry stalks.

THYME *Thymus* species
Plant type: Perennial

Wild thyme is said to be a favorite of the fairies. One of the ancient strewing herbs that were placed on floors to cleanse the air, thyme has antiseptic qualities, and in fact, it's name may be derived from a Greek term meaning "to fumigate." It also has a long history of treating respiratory disorders.

Thyme

Uses. Thyme is a versatile herb with a mild resinous flavor, typically included in both *bouquet garni* and *fines herbes* blends. It's culinary use extends throughout the kitchen, including meat, fish, eggs, cheese, and vegetables.

In the garden. Thyme is a low-growing, perennial evergreen shrub. Some varieties grow in low mats on the ground; others may reach 15 inches. They all have small, rounded leaves and tiny flowers in shades of white, pink, and purple that appear in early summer. Buy several transplants or make divisions from mature plants. Place plants in full sun in well-drained soil, allowing 9 to 12 inches between plants.

There are at least 200 thyme cultivars, many of which are landscaping plants, but many others have culinary value. English thyme *(T. vulgaris)* is the standard; golden lemon thyme *(T.* × *citriodorus)* is also excellent. *T. herba-baronna,* the caraway thyme, was used to season the great roasts of beef ("barons" of beef) in feudal times. Scratch and sniff leaves before purchasing, if possible. *Zones 4–9.*

Harvesting and preserving. Clip fresh sprigs as needed, or harvest the entire plant to about 2 inches from the ground. Thymes dry easily and retain good flavor. Hang-dry sprigs just before buds appear.

HERBAL
Resources

SUPPLIERS OF FRESH AND DRIED HERBS

Diamond Organics
P.O. Box 2159
Freedom, CA 95019
Phone: 888-ORGANIC
Fax: 888-888-6777
e-mail: shop@diamondorganics.com
Web site: www.diamondorganics.com
Fresh organic herbs and edible flowers (fruits and vegetables, as well) airshipped overnight

Adriana's Caravan
409 Vanderbilt Street
Brooklyn, NY 11218
Phone: 800-316-0820
e-mail: Adricara@aol.com
Web site: www.adrianascaravan.com
Dried herbs and spices as well as international condiments, coffees, and teas

AmeriHerb, Inc.
P.O. Box 1968
Ames, IA 50010
Phone: 800-267-6141
Fax: 515-232-8615
Dried herbs and spices in wholesale quantities

Mountain Rose Herbs
20818 High Street
North San Juan, CA 95960
Phone: 800-879-3337
Fax: 530-292-9138
Web site: www.botanical.com/mtrose/
Dried herbs, botanicals, and seasonings, as well as herb seeds, teas, and bodycare products

Penzey's Spices
P.O. Box 933
Muskego, WI 53150
Phone: 414-679-7207
Fax: 414-679-7207
e-mail: eblon@execpc.com
Web site: www.penzeys.com
Dried herbs, spices, and gourmet herb blends

SUPPLIERS OF HERB SEEDS AND PLANTS

Abundant Life Seed Foundation
P.O. Box 7722, 930 Lawrence Street
Port Townsend, WA 98368-0772
Phone: 360-385-5660
Fax: 360-385-7455
Nonprofit educational foundation committed to raising and collecting open-pollinated cultivars

The Cook's Garden
P.O. Box 535
Londonderry, VT 05148-0535
Phone: 802-824-3400
Fax: 800-457-9705
e-mail: www@cooksgarden.com
Web site: www.cooksgarden.com

Johnny's Selected Seeds
R.R. 1, Box 2580
Foss Hill Road
Albion, ME 04910-9731
Phone: 207-437-9294
Fax: 207-437-2165
e-mail: staff@johnnyseeds.com
Web site: www.johnnyseeds.com

147

Nichols Garden Nursery
1190 N. Pacific Highway
Albany, OR 97321-4580
Phone: 541-928-9280
Fax: 541-967-8406
e-mail: info@gardennursery.com
Web site: www.gardennursery.com

George W. Park Seed Company
1 Parkton Avenue
Greenwood, SC 29647-0001
Phone: 800-845-3366
Fax: 800-209-0360
e-mail: info@parkseed.com
Web site: www.parkseed.com

Pinetree Garden Seeds
P.O. Box 300, 616A Lewiston Road
New Gloucester, ME 04260
Phone: 207-926-4112
Fax: 888-527-3337
e-mail: superseeds@worldnet.att.net
Web site: www.superseeds.com

Redwood City Seed Company
P.O. Box 361
Redwood City, CA 94064
Phone: 650-325-7333

The Sandy Mush Herb Nursery
316 Surrett Cove Road
Leicester, NC 28748-5517
Phone: 828-683-2014

Seed Savers Exchange
3094 North Winn Road
Decorah, IA 52101
Phone: 319-382-5990

Southern Exposure Seed Exchange
P.O. Box 170
Earlysville, VA 22936
Phone: 804-973-4703
Fax: 804-973-8717
e-mail:
gardens@southernexposure.com
Web site:
www.southernexposure.com

The Thyme Garden
20546 Alsea Highway
Alsea, OR 97324
Phone: 541-487-8671
Fax: 541-487-8671
e-mail: thymegarden@proaxis.com
Web site: www.thymegarden.com

Well-Sweep Farm
205 Mount Bethel Road
Port Murray, NJ 07865
Phone: 908-852-5390
Fax: 908-852-1649

ORGANIC GARDENING SUPPLIES

Gardener's Supply Company
128 Intervale Road
Burlington, VT 05401
Phone: 800-863-1700
Fax: 802-863-3501
e-mail: info@gardeners.com
Web site: www.gardeners.com

Gardens Alive!
5100 Schenley Place
Lawrenceburg, IN 47025
Phone: 812-537-8698
Fax: 812-537-5108
e-mail: gardenhelp@gardens-alive.com
Web site: www.gardens-alive.com

The Natural Gardening Company
217 San Anselmo Avenue
San Anselmo, CA 94960
Phone: 707-766-9303
Fax: 707-766-9747
Web site: www.naturalgardening.com

Peaceful Valley Farm Supply
P.O. Box 2209
110 Spring Hill Drive, #2
Grass Valley, CA 95945
Phone: 888-784-1722
Fax: 530-272-4794
Web site: www.groworganic.com

Books on Herbs

Barton, Barbara J. *Gardening by Mail.* Boston: Houghton Mifflin Company, 1997.

Beston, Henry. *Herbs and the Earth.* Boston: David R. Godine, 1990.

Foster, Gertrude B., and Rosemary F. Louden. *Park's Success with Herbs.* Greenwood, SC: George W. Park Seed Company, 1980.

James, Tina (with Barbara Steele and Marlene Lufrui). *The Salad Bar in Your Own Backyard.* Reisterstown, MD: Gardening from the Heart (12812 Bridlepath Road, Reisterstown, MD 21136), 1990.

Kowalchik, Claire, and William H. Hylton, editors. *Rodale's Illustrated Encyclopedia of Herbs.* Emmaus, PA: Rodale Press, 1987.

McClure, Susan. *The Herb Gardener: A Guide for All Seasons.* Pownal, VT: Storey Communications, Inc., 1996.

Robson, Nancy Taylor. *Oldfield Lamb Cookbook.* Galena, MD: Buttonwood Press (Box 74, Galena, MD 21635), 1990.

Saville, Carole. *Exotic Herbs: A Compendium of Exceptional Culinary Herbs.* New York: Henry Holt and Company, 1997.

Smith, Miranda. *Your Backyard Herb Garden.* Emmaus, PA: Rodale Press, 1999.

Sombke, Laurence. *Beautiful Easy Herbs: How to Get the Most from Herbs in Your Garden and in Your Home.* Emmaus, PA: Rodale Press, 1997.

Magazines on Herbs

The Herb Companion
Interweave Press
201 East Fourth Street, Dept. 0-B
Loveland, CO 80537-5655
Phone: 800-456-6018
Fax: 970-667-8317
e-mail: HerbCompanion@hcpress.com
Web site: www.interweave.com

The Herb Quarterly
P.O. Box 689
San Anselmo, CA 94960
Phone: 415-455-9540
Fax: 415-455-9541
e-mail: HerbQuart@aol.com
Web site: www.herbquarterly.com

Rodale's Essential Herbal Handbooks

If you enjoyed *Cooking with Herbs,* you will also enjoy:
Herbal Remedies by Kathleen Fisher
Herbal Home Hints by Louise Gruenberg

Acknowledgments

Thanks to Barbara Weiland for listening and especially to Gwen Steege for lighting the path.

Index

Page references in **bold** indicate tables.